CW00347130

# STREET CRHYMES

## JUSTIN ROLLINS

**Street Crhymes**
Justin Rollins

**ISBN** 978-1-904380-99-3 (Paperback)
**ISBN** 978-1-908162-65-6 (Kindle/Epub ebook)
**ISBN** 978-1-908162-66-3 (Adobe ebook)

**Copyright** © 2014 This work is the copyright of Justin Rollins. All intellectual property and associated rights are hereby asserted and reserved by him in full compliance with UK, European and international law. No part of this book may be copied, reproduced, stored in any retrieval system or transmitted in any form or by any means, including in hard copy or via the internet, without the prior written permission of the publishers to whom all such rights have been assigned worldwide.

**Cover design** © 2014 Waterside Press. Design by www.gibgob.com

**Main UK distributor** Gardners Books, 1 Whittle Drive, Eastbourne, East Sussex, BN23 6QH. Tel: +44 (0)1323 521777; sales@gardners.com; www.gardners.com

**North American distribution** Ingram Book Company, One Ingram Blvd, La Vergne, TN 37086, USA. Tel: (+1) 615 793 5000; inquiry@ingramcontent.com

**Cataloguing-In-Publication Data** A catalogue record for this book can be obtained from the British Library.

**Printed by** CPI Group (UK) Ltd, Croydon, CR0 4YY.

**e-book** *Street Crhymes* is available as an ebook and also to subscribers of Myilibrary, Dawsonera, ebrary, and Ebscohost.

**Published 2014 by**
Waterside Press Ltd.
Sherfield Gables
Sherfield on Loddon
Hook, Hampshire
United Kingdom RG27 0JG


**Telephone** +44(0)1256 882250
**E-mail** enquiries@watersidepress.co.uk
**Online catalogue** WatersidePress.co.uk

# Street Crhymes

## Justin Rollins

**WATERSIDE** PRESS

# Table of Contents

# About the Author

**Justin Rollins** is the author of *The Lost Boyz* (2011) a true account of graffiti-gangs and disaffected youth, acclaimed by people working with hard to reach young people. It tells of life on the streets of London from a young age and the hazards this entailed from drugs, alcohol, self-harm and mental health issues, leading in the author's case to incarceration in a young offender institution.

Since then Justin Rollins has turned his life around and helps young people to do the same, mainly through his writings and live performances of his work.

# Acknowledgements

Helen Taylor, Noel Razor Smith, David Boomah Williams, Debbie Howes, Danny Cassius Conner, Daniel Campbell, James Byrne, Joe Girton, Simon Bishop, Vicky Gilligan, Tommy Lanzarote, Gary Mets Butler, Yolande Bavan, The Thirst, Simon CD Man Scott, Sharon Rollins, Sean London, Darron J Connett and Tyler Brain.

# What others say about Justin Rollins

'When I met Justin Rollins, approximately 13 years ago in a Sutton Youth Club he was confused, angry, bitter and struggling to communicate with everyone around him. It was clear to me that underneath the bravado and the tough talk he was just a nice young person like many others but he was struggling to comprehend his own identity; as some children from mixed parentage do.

I met Justin at the point where his offending behaviour was coming to the notice of the local Youth Offending Team and I was assigned as his Key Worker. We got on well but he was determined to do what he wanted regardless of what anyone said or did to deter him.

It wasn't long before Justin had slipped so far into criminal activity that he was beyond my reach and he became yet another statistic in the Youth Justice System. I was upset and felt we had lost another young person and this story was becoming too familiar in my field.

Imagine my surprise when years later Mr Rollins contacted me to say he was an author, a father and though he did get heavily involved in crime he had completely turned his life around! Justin has defied all the adversities that life has thrown at him and is now educating others through his writing.

"Street Crhymes" reveals what goes on in the mind of a young offender, how they really feel and provides some real home truths about life behind bars. Young people, parents and individuals working with at risk young people will definitely benefit from reading this as it is gives you an idea of what you may be faced with and can be a great tool to help you respond to youth at risk of offending behaviour':

**David A Williams, Director of Youth Services, London Urban Arts Academy**

'Justin Rollins is THE authentic poetic voice of the streets. His rhymes and stanzas flow out from the page like a wave of ghetto 'hoodies' on a mission to open your mind and force you to think. Gritty urban realism, the plaintive cries of disaffected youth and a stinging humour that can make you laugh or cry in equal measure are his milieu. His words can be as sharp and icy cold as a dagger to the heart, or as hot as a blast from a £50 shotgun, but always knowing, like the sly wink of a magistrate who is about to send you down for a long time. He is bringing a message and whether you like it or not it is real. Truly a genuine voice of the lost generation':

**Noel 'Razor' Smith, Author of** *A Few Kind Words and A Loaded Gun*

'Justin Rollins has a remarkable ability. His poems spring not from agonising over a blank sheet of paper, but almost instantly, in full-flow. This makes for fresh, spontaneous and original work (even if readers of his autobiographical *The Lost Boyz* may recognise some of the landmarks). Full of telling imagery, unorthodox thinking, clandestine adventures and a sense of the absurd, this is life through the lens of someone who has overcome setbacks, discrimination and a bleak past. With creativity in his veins and a determination to improve life, Rollins' work merits study by anyone interested in youth culture and hallmarks of personal change.'

**Bryan Gibson, Director, Waterside Press**

'Transformation of a beleaguered mind and body giving rise to and embracing the artistic creative spirit. Resurrection!'

**Yolande Bavan, Jazz Legend**

'The poems in this book represent the London street life of many young adolescents that have no guidance, no positive role models and no sense of community as they have been shunned from society. Blinded and brainwashed by the system, it is our mission to break free from these invisible mental shackles and rise up.

It's really inspiring to see someone who we know and have roamed the streets with in our youth doing something with his talent and sharing his experiences in a positive way. Justin Rollins is a very talented wordsmith who paints pictures with topics most don't want to talk about.

Make a difference, be different, build, create, inspire and live free.'

**The Thirst, London-based rock band and peers of the author (see thethirst.co.uk)**

Dedicated to Daisy and Gabriella

In loving memory of
Jamaine Taylor
1981-2013

# THE DARK STREETS

## Streets of Crhyme

What's your vision?
For me it's like kids are stuck in a prison
Or a position
Where they are hooded-up
And can't make the transition
It's like they carry weight and more
Like middle-eastern children
Carrying weaponry in war

Tell me why the youth have no ambition
Gold tooth, attitude and no one listens

It could have been so easy
But the streets tempt and tease
This lost breed

A nine-to-five seems a dead-end
When diamonds and ice are the in trend
So robberies get carried out through greed
Digital scales weigh up potent weed
Sold for hundreds and fifties
Standing on the corner looking shifty

Kids asking friends
'If I went jail would you miss me?'

It's a cold game
Where the evil gain
Where needles drain away the pain

'Cause this is the Streets of Crhyme
Every kid screaming 'The streets are mine'
Until they're lost and locked
Serving Big Time

Did an old lag
Try to educate a young lad?
Did that young lad
Turn real bad?

Does he shed a tear
Alone when he's ticking off years?
Is it a brave face
Or does he really have no fear?

I don't know
But you don't wanna live here!

## Karma

I was sitting in the vehicle gazing
Surrounded by Hell blazing
Trouble up the road I was facing

I was a lost man, a mother's lost son
Brainwashed by the 'live by the gun'
Mentality
But a gangster's life is just a fallacy

An illusion
That has our kids stuck in confusion
Self-abusing

Programmed by music videos
Filled with nice cars and fast girls
The entrapments of this fast world

The seven deadly sins are being played out
You have to question
What you are really about

Cocaine cowboys
Scarface fantasies
Wannabes
Like X-Factor hopefuls
There ain't no going back
Feel the rope pull
I've been there stuck in that daydream
But that dream is really a nightmare
Like when demons collide
You will feel a chill down your spine

Destiny is a choice we all have
Like when a dad leaves his child and never looks back
Selfish souls may forever perish
When it's material evil you truly cherish

Sometimes your actions come back and bite
So whilst you sip champagne in the dead of night
With that half-naked lady in your sight
Just remember the Devil will follow you
Until you put your actions right!

## The Devil's Nest

The streets have stolen a million men
Grinning whilst sinning and then

At their darkest hour screaming regret
They gambled with death like Russian roulette

You see a selfish heart shall perish alone
Like a king knocked from his throne

Like a bird with a damaged wing
One day a thief will account for his sins

I don't mean in a biblical sense
    or in a mythical way
But most bad men in history have paid

Paid the price for living a life of
Crime
Plush cars, diamond ice in their prime
On the other side
Is a life of grime
Blood-money will have you butchered like swine

Playing with fire will have you burnt
Lessons in life you'll never learn

Churning in a pot, boiling in hell
Paying eternally for the pain the rest felt

In the Devil's Nest you will forever dwell.

'Cause the true key to living is forgiving and love
While these men walk not giving a
Fuck
Even the biggest one day come unstuck
Found slumped and gunned down
In the back of a truck

## Teenage Flashbacks

Remember those Morden days
Sun shining as we paint raze

Walking tracks with chromes and blacks
Wax oils and Simoniz chromes
Those rails were our homes

1999 was our time to shine
706 Baf Let WZ

Did those paint fumes go to our heads
'Cos Baf, now you and London graff is dead

Permanent markers and permanent memories
But now those rails are empty

Where have you gone?
From graff to psychically fighting through a storm
Yet through my writing once again you're born

I can smell the brew, ink and barbecue blacks
As I march through this flashback

WZ and WK collide
The Northern Line we ride
It's 'Tales From The Track Side'!

## Not Perfect

They call her Miss Holloway
'Cause that's where she spends most of her days
Like a revolving door
She's back and forth
She's back in rehab
Another course
Deep therapy sessions to find the source
Of her problems
But it won't stop them

Though she tries so hard
It's like how do you erase these childhood scars
There's thousands more trapped behind bars

Doors rotating
She's free again
Drinking on the square with her Alkie friends

It's the Asbo lady
Pissed up and crazy
I see you out my window
Analyse how you flow

I wonder what happened
I've seen the black eyes
Seen you saddened

There's thousands like you
On this cold-arsed planet
They judge you like you planned it
That liquor has you stranded

I hear the screaming and the cursing
Seen your situation worsen
I wonder if it's all worth it

It's like I'm judging you too
I guess I'm not perfect.

## Tales from the Crypt

This city is full of ghosts and ghouls
Locked in The Clink
Tortured with tools
Where Jack the Ripper ruled

Haunted museums and eerie schools
Necropolis Railway
The smell of death
Caped figure with alcohol breath

Can you hear those footsteps
Creeping-up slowly?
I don't know if these ghosts are holy

It's enough to bring goosebumps
Enough to bring shivers
Another body floating down the river

This city is full of shadows
This city is full of tales
The stench of rotten bodies
Witness the smell

Poltergeists fuelled by rage
Been stalking this station since the days of the plague

Commuting
The stress that you feel
Sometimes in that tunnel you start to get chills
That was the Blind Beggar emptying tills

You hear babies crying
The echoes are not stopping
Ghosts jumping for cover
As German bombs keep dropping

A tour of this ghouls' town
Don't be disarmed
Visions of Kings Cross fire alarm

Look around you
A billion walked these roads
Sweating on the tube
But somewhat cold

This isn't a history class
But you are still learning
London tales have your stomach
    churning
347 years later London's still burning.

## Graffiti-eyes

The writing's on the wall
But these fools don't understand it
We creep and come prepared like a bandit
Work late at night and end up stranded

Missed the night train
'Cos we just hit it with bright paint

The smell of solvents is going to my head
Now I'm walking railways instead
When I should of really been tucked-up in bed
With a cuddly toy called Ted

But I'm hitting every electrical box
My name hits and drips
Spraying our gang names like 'Bloods' and 'Crips'
The London skyline from a hidden view
Painting trains with my villain crew

What's it all about and who is Banksy?
He's not from this world and I'll say it frankly
Stealing paint and brew
Has us moving cranky

Feel the breeze from the night train
Feel the buzz through my hyped brain
Surfing trains like a roller coaster
Lucky to not get burnt
Like bread in a toaster
We advertise
Just like a fly-poster

Getting chased
By the Transport Police branch
Has *us* hiding in trees
Holding onto *our* branch

Or in a bush for half the night
Until the German Shepherds
Are out of sight
Eyes stinging from the morning light

My name's going city wide
See my tags stained on the outside
And inside of this tube
Whilst we ride
Just a small glimpse through my
    graffiti-eyes.

## Anger Management

This demon in my face
Outside my space
With my child screaming

Those prison years made me raw
Left my baby child on the floor
That cold pavement

Run into my house to grab my blade
Ready to put this demon in his grave

How dare you bring the war
With my baby daughter by my side
Now you made her cry
Now you have to die

Like cartoons running in circles
If I caught you the knife would hurt you
Piercing your flesh
Death was lingering
My hands were tingling

I don't need to lie or brag
I've been chopped-up and stabbed
Left others bleeding on slabs
Been hunted by killers
Lived a horror, walked a thriller

They say 'Love thy neighbour'
What about love thy stranger?
'Cos he took that blade
And saved you from danger

I would have committed murder
A father's journey would have gone no further

I was a killer, my finger just never pulled
    the trigger

Now six years later
I'm thinking of this hater
Looking at my daughter
Eyes dropping salty water

Looking at my reflection
Baby girl, I'm your protection
So glad the neighbour snatched the
    weapon
A dark road I was stepping
But I learnt from harsh lessons
Now this is my confession

I always swore revenge on that demon
Fantasised on seeing him
Bleeding
His mother dressed in black screaming

But I let it go
And I started to breathe
Started to see
Stick the knife in and leave
No that life is no longer for me.

## Live by the Sword

Quick living
Splashing dirty cash is unforgiving
Not realising you're slipping
Too busy shopping-tripping

You're on fire
Mercedes stamp on your tyre
A world full of crooks and liars
Police ear-wigging down a wire

Firearms, sparks flying
Ears ringing
Heartbeat pounding and singing
Off beat to the rhythm
Reputation has now risen
Only fast cash in your vision
No mercy on this mission

Take off the mask
Rehydrate through the water flask
Adrenalin come down
Sirens echo through this ghost town

Forensics looking for the weapon
It's a rocky path you're stepping
Looking through pipes and drains
Finding knives that have inflicted pain
Round here it's all the same
Just another yellow sign in the game
But who's to blame?

Now the enemies circle
Another group want to hurt you
Bullets flirt with you
Look in the mirror that's you!
A vicious cycle

Like a boxer once again losing his title
A Teflon vest is vital
Or you'll get taken out like Michael

But this ain't the Jackson Five
This is London where it's hard to survive
When you live a life
Where gun violence is rife

It's a small world
There are many dead ends
Some friends will not sleep until they
    seek revenge
It's like digging a grave and filling it with
    cement
Killing another, leaves death's stench

So it's lights out now
There's no time to repent.

## Street Horses

I remember knock-down Ginger
On the local streets we would linger

It was all simple then
Back when
We would knock for Ms Mental
She would chase us up the road
Take off and go mental

We would climb along garage roofs
Annoying kids with a sweet tooth

Running from the shop with a Ribena
The shopkeeper hunting us like a hyaena
But like Bolt we were sprinters
Climbing
Fingers getting pricked by splinters
Stinging nettles and brambles
Wheelies
Holding onto bike handles
Grew a bit older and became vandals

Stare into the eyes of a lost child
Running through miles of dry grass
As fast as the gipsy horses grazing this field
The sun blazing upon these hills

If I could jump upon this horse and calm him
'Here boy, here boy!'
Don't alarm him

I'd ride my local streets
All the boys on their bikes would be jealous of me
And I'm running and riding this horse
Like a stunt man
If anyone can do a stunt I can

Like this journey was all planned

One day I'd ride these alleys and dips
Past my graffiti tags that drip

My horse is like the guiding light
Like that bit of hope in the dead of night

Me and my horse would really test them
Something out of a black and white western
But my name ain't John and my name ain't Wayne
Now my eleven-year-old heart's in pain

'Cause those horses are gone
Vanished, banished away
Today I'm on a rampage
Filled with menace I wander these blocks
See the hardest villain stop and watch
He stared into the eyes of an eleven-year-old
Then shivered because the glare was so cold
I feel like I could flip cars
Rip bars from mean fences
The streets better prepare for a teenage menace! *

*A video clip of the author reading Street Horses can
be viewed at WatersidePress.co.uk/StreetHorses*

## Gang Bang Slang

Forget Little Bo Peep
It's Death Row on these streets
We call a feud beef
Even if it's minor

Now minor means little
But don't get it twisted
You can still see the pistol

For something so petty
Brains splashed across the road like spaghetti
Gunpowder falling like confetti

Better wear a bully
Now that means a vest
Protect your chest
Protect your neck
Better protect your rep

Now that means reputation
So don't be singing down the station
Singing doesn't mean Whitney Houston
It means refusing to follow the code
The code of the road
Means not talking to the police
And selling your soul
Or you'll be dwelling in a hole

Get rich or die trying
Nosey neighbours prying
Keep your chin up, don't look away
Those crooks will seek you out today

Don't look that way
The Mandem are straight road

Now that means their respected
And cold

Let me jump in this whip and fly to the junction
A whip is a car
Do you get my induction?

You see kids want to be streetwise
Like it's big or clever
Want the cars and the jewels to look fresher
But believe me there is always a robber ready to severe
So you and your friends better stick together

Only the hardcore will make it
One out of a hundred, it's basic
It's not glamorous so don't fake it
'Cause knife wounds leave people deflated!

## Welcome to the Jungle

Burnt out cars
Broken windows
Metal bars, childhood scars

Barking dogs
Sirens blaring
Patrolling youths hooded-up scaring
Not caring

CCTV recording
Nosey neighbours reporting
Doors kicked off hinges
Play areas full of syringes

*Big Issue* sellers
And beggars

Broke terrors
To get the cash
Take it to desperate measures

Saw dust covering blood
If all goes wrong in God we trust
Staring up to the heavens
Getting out is a must
Graffiti on walls covered in dust

It's a jungle out here
And I'm welcoming you
You could call it Hell
Or an urban zoo
Come live here for a week
And you'll know this is true.

## The Cycle

Daddy never gave a shit
Too busy down the pub snorting sniff
Wishing his girlfriend had aborted it
Just another baby born into all this

No father figure for this beautiful girl
How it would affect her only time would tell
Violence in the home
Contained in a child's dome
Seeing her mother knocked from her throne

At times that young girl felt alone
School was a comedy like 'Live at the Apollo'
Seeing mummy beaten was hard to swallow
And though she hated her dad
In his footsteps she followed

She bullied other kids
Made them feel degraded
Lost in this mind-set her parents created
Social services with no clue what to do
So like a thousand others, they lost track of you

Sofa surfing
Boyfriends cursing
Now it's black eyes she's nursing

It's a vicious roundabout
With few twists and turns
Sitting with a photo of her daddy
With a lighter she burns

So she's out on the concrete
And she wants revenge
Now she's leader of a girl gang
Just her and her friends

Losing control rapidly
Whilst with her new family
Searching for love and searching for peace
But all she can find is deceit on those streets
Abused by these men again and again
Though she lies to herself like they're her boyfriends
Some twisted fantasy like they're making love
But that man who's on top is another thug
They push her about and push her with drugs
She sells and smokes
And pukes up her guts

Got to pick your friends wisely
'Cause many move slyly
Eyes open and watch who's around you
Now she's locked in HMP Downview.

### Music Affects

Everybody wanna live a 2pac destiny
Unloading there strap 'til
It's empty
But the truth is
You live a life of pain that's ruthless
And when you die only a few cry
And ask why
Self-destructing screaming thug life
But in reality it's a mug's life
Those flowers by your grave turning brown
Petals falling to the ground
Stinging nettles surround
Screaming
'How long will they morn me?'
Not for long ......
'Cause life goes on.

# FOOTPRINTS ON MEMORY LANE

## Morden

Morden was the town we rose from
Now it's all gone
Gotta stay strong

Graffiti tag spraying
But now our names are fading

And I'm hurting
On how my boys are deserting
What were those days worth?

Thirty gang members
'Warriors for life'
I stand by that saying
But many were just playing
Playing with poisonous cards
Trying to erase
Those childhood scars
I wouldn't trust many
With a pound or penny
Now most cannot enter my realm
Only time will tell

I walk on our memories
I walk within our shadows
I can feel our childhood energies
Brush past me

I find it slightly hard
Walking through this town
But somehow feel safe
Somehow feel some strange sense

Some turned to God
Others to drugs
Others to drinking in pubs
Others getting lost in clubs
Some kicking cell doors
Sectioned under the Mental Health Act
Dribbling on floors

If I could go back I would for a
Minute
Put all of my knowledge in it
Show my friends different paths
Steer them from danger
Now I look in your eyes and we're
    strangers

We called it the War Zone
Morden town was once my home

But you hold
So much darkness
Harshness
It's like I can no longer
Hold you
Walk through you
Trust you

Morden Morden where have you gone?
Morden Morden don't come back
'Cause the time has come
To walk our separate tracks.

## Welcome to Tooting

These walls are deaf to sirens
The people who live here
Are fierce like lions
They wouldn't help you
If you were crying

Alkies drinking their lives away
Lost their wives along the way
Edward VII statue
Standing like it was brand new
Nobody notices his presence
As they exit the tube

Be on your guard
Even the businessmen in this town
Are hard
Concrete jungle,
We're swinging on trees
Preacher in the high street
Down on his knees

The smell off spices in the air
Mixed with pollution
Visitors stop and stare
Looking through my stained glass
A whole family live in boxes
Out there on the grass
Polish drunks and Tamils too
My manor
Is like a multi-cultural zoo

Scary to an onlooker's vision
Drained faces,
Like the residents
Are stuck in prison
But the middle-class take over has risen

Pubs bulldozed
Luxury flats appearing
Ancient residents disappearing
Has got the locals fearing
That their exit is nearing

Like Drouet's Paupers Child Asylum
Kids in my manor
Are still dying
Has much changed
From the mid-19th century
Ghosts of 118 kids
Can you feel the energy

In my town full of footprints
These ghouls
Will make your foot sprint
Send a shiver
You can find us deep down
South of the river

You may of seen us in summer
Out here looting
Noisy red buses polluting
Another kid stabbed
Another shooting
This is my manor
Welcome to Tooting.

## A Million Mordens

I used to walk this path in another life
My footprints can still be witnessed

My words are stained upon dusty walls
Those goosebumps were me walking
    through your present

Leaves blew in the wind
They formed my figure

Though I'm from a different realm
Somehow you feel the shiver

A million worlds but we just don't see
Birds flew away

The breeze swayed those trees
Though my body is not the same

My consciousness is
I'm wiser

I'm older
I drop change to the beggar

Sitting outside the station
Though a million trains have passed

He's still waiting
I knew I'd come back

I knew I was curious
Curiosity

I smelt these streets in a million dreams
I rose to my feet

I tried to talk
But could not speak

Why are my friends not talking to me
I mumble

I shout
I stutter

A million times I walked
Through this gutter

You see when a photo is taken
It leaves fingerprints on the soul
So when that soul is set free
It may visit that photo for eternity.

# IT'S ALL POLITICAL

## Tragedy

I was born in a mining town
Where there were no jobs
Some moved to Manchester to steal
And rob

I heard Billy's doing well, living a life so swell
He's got the car, got the pin-up girl
But I refuse to bow down to criminality
And I swear to you it's testing my sanity
So I break my back twenty-four-seven
Then it all changed after 9-11

I'm a soldier, I'm a soldier
This was my way out, my way to escape
Camouflage gear, get me out of this place

When I saluted the general I felt a source of pride
A feeling I had never felt inside
What more could I want
With my friends and guns?

We were the sons of our nation
Fighting for freedom
the war I was now facing
I was going on tour
I had found my placement
A band of brothers together
In the dusty roads, under hot weather
Sharing our daily bread
Looking out for the ragheads

If we'd never joined most would've become skag heads
In coffins, brown bread
But we were shooting terrorists instead

Or that's what I thought
Until I saw women and kids die
That could've been my family
And it hurts inside
I remember some locals kidnapped a Yank
And set him on fire along with his tank

They screamed they wanted revenge
In the name if their Lord
We're fighting with machine-guns
They're fighting with swords
Sticks and stones
US missiles and secret drones

They never told me I'd be fighting for this
But some of the boys don't care, they have a death wish
It came way too quick
Two of our platoon blown to bits
By a suicide bomb set off by a kid

My friends seek revenge
They killed his 12-year-old friend
Up close and personal
They say black out the madness
Or it will worsen you
How do you stay sane with a nation cursing you?

Somehow I survived the killing and the lies
Our Government had blinded my eyes
You see those people were human
And they died like dogs
It was a war about oil not about gods

Now I'm mentally scarred
From seeing bodies blown-up and charred
This alcohol will have me locked behind bars

I feel used and abused and see no way out
The drugs ain't working with no loved ones about
You see I entered a war
But my biggest battle is me

Sometimes I feel like I'm floating
There is no gravity
That war wasn't fair
It was a tragedy!

## Risen

London city
This zoo is split in two

High rises
Pit bulls with muzzles

Builders' tools getting rusty
No work in this struggle

Normal men are forced to
Hustle

Benefits chopped
But where are those jobs
They say crime figures are down
But people are out on the rob

Music videos promoting wealth
Do the watchers know real richness is health
But out here in the 'big smoke'
Life is no joke
You will not last a day being broke

Who said these streets are paved with gold?
You're either a slave on a low wage

Or signing on the dole
When that dole money vanishes
Anger boils
And could explode like canisters
You better hold onto life's banisters

Through these harsh times
Need money quick so people commit fast crimes

Paying to drive through your own city is shitty
When it's still congested
Live by the rules or face being arrested
They are cutting A&Es and police numbers too
Seat-belts on as a depression looms
People turn to drugs, brain cells go boom
Suicides are up, to escape the gloom

You see the rich don't even eat the same food
They live in greenery not in this concrete tomb

Take my words as a lesson
You have to stay strong to escape this depression
I can understand the next man's aggression
Being played out in this man-made recession

Education is the way to success
The only way to see you out of this mess
May I confess
The system nearly broke me in the midst of this test
But I rose, my chin up and pushed out my chest

Like a blind man that had a vision
Deep thinkers will escape this prison

March forward, remain driven
Never give up until your goals have arisen.

## Clues for Politicians

Weak get played off against strong
Strong against weak
Plastic surgery
Fake hips, lips and cheeks
Self-image turning people into freaks

Rich against poor
Poor against rich
High rise dungeons
Life is a bitch
Mansions, caviar
BMW car,
Jet set trip way afar

Burnt out vehicles
Yobs on the prowl
It's enough to make you throw in the towel
Three kids to feed, but not enough food
Benefits cut
Snobs looking down at you

Treat the Brixton residents like lice
Ship them out to Croydon
And whack up house prices
A gang offers hope
Like some other way to cope
Make a little money from selling coke

The system has you trapped
Like a rat down a hole
No work, no signing on the dole
Locked-up for years
Now out on parole

Ministers stop talking shit
Whilst you sit on your thrones

You call this the pits
We call this place home

You would never
Could never walk in these shoes
Controlling people through the news
Well I have news for you
You don't know how we live
But this should give a clue!

## Funny Money

People die for it
Others cry for it
Break backs for just a little bit
Piss it up the pub wall
Lay in bed depressed
Wishing they had saved it
Some swim in it
Were born with it
Think they are better
Because of it
Many don't care for it
They feel rich without it
Many can't do without it
If they have it they will let you know about it
Throw it in the air and shout it
Some just can't attract it
Forever moaning
Groaning for it
People change because of it
Like a squirrel they won't share it
They bury it
And hide it
I'll ask you something about it
Can it bring happiness?
If you took it from the rich
It would bring them sadness
Give it to the poor
They would show gladness
Let me ask you something else about it
If everyone in town
Entered their bank
And demanded to withdraw their cash
Every bank door would be locked in a flash
Because they have not got it

So tell me something
How could they have lost it?
Situation is cold and frosty
Recession is a state of mind
Because I think you will find
How do you lose digits from a screen
This nation is blind!

### Cameron's Kids

They say you're innocent until proven guilty
But it's the other way around
Police stop and search in this town
Racial profiling
Empty your pockets

They drive off smiling
Nosy neighbours looking on
Police tactics cooking up a storm

We throw stones and bottles too
Police scratch off their numbers and throttle you
We get brainwashed by videos
Then go out and loot
Stolen goods get sold for a third of the price
Then we buy herbs and smoke up the spice
They call us Chavs and council house scum
You think his language is bad
Hear his foul mouthed mum

See we wasn't born with riches
Luxury food on tap
No we called our teachers bitches
Became one of the chaps
I was born guilty
Brought up in those flats

So when you drive on by
Just give us a bib
Cameron what would you do
If this was your kid?

## Needy Streets

Back in this ghost town
Where most drown
Some sell powder for greed
To buy material things they don't need
Dealings go wrong and some bleed
It all goes on in the life they lead

Lead, lead
Pit bull dogs get walked on leads
And chrome chains
Anger blows like propane
Kids walk a one-way lane
Dog attacks on the rise
Prisons are packed inside

Inside, inside
Get inside the mind of a villain
Ask him why blood is spilling
Ask the government why prisons are filling
Why lies are spread
Why police hardly get convicted
And their lives are spared

Spared, spared
Tell me who's got a spare key
I'll head to Feltham and set some kids free
Sit them down and give them therapy
Take them out of the ghetto
Give them opportunities
So I beg you please

Stop the kids killing kids
It's a disease
The streets look like the result of a
    stampede
A little peace is all we need

It's what we need
It's what we need.

## 'Bye Phone

This effing iPhone
I wanna scream "Bye phone'
I'm not gonna lie phone
Sometimes I don't want you in my home

Just relaxing, just lying alone
Ringer-ding-ding
It's my effing phone

How the Hell can I nap
When my head's polluted by apps

So I'm up till break of dawn
Twitter, Facebook
You're making me yawn

iPhone equals rotten apple
All you do is babble

Like troops invading my castle
I feel I want to get my hammer out and
     blast you

Instagram making us nosey
With my fifty-one-ten
Life was rosy
Lying here trying to get cosy

But FaceTime is attacking me
I don't wanna talk
Stop harassing me

Emails you're making me mad
But now my chick's bought an iPad

Temple Run you have me addicted
I'm not working, I'm jumping ditches

And speeding through tunnels
I'm like sand draining through funnels

Look around you
Glued to phones, no communicating
Social networks have us hating

Mucking with our concentration
A step towards a robotic nation.

## Total Eclipse

We invade countries and call them terrorists
I think these puppets needs to visit therapists

It's all war
It's all propaganda
Child soldiers armed in Uganda

But our western television
Is blinding our vision
We stick our thumbs up to their decisions

But my thumbs are down
And I throw rotten food
Because I will never bow down to you

I couldn't care less if you're Muslim or Jew or a Christian
I just want you all to listen
We're all one
All stuck in this global prison
While you watch your fuzzy box
Eating microwaved crap

Kids are being slayed in the back
A million men pray on mats

Or on creaky benches in chapels
Wondering why Adam ate the apple

To me it's all muddled
Now the puddles are rising

Humanity is sliding
But are the people who are deciding
What gets programmed into our minds
in total eclipse?
We are the walking blind.

### Handling Hair

Bald-headed women
Robbed of their looks
By hungry crooks
The world just shook

Bald-headed women
Robbed for their hair
See the horror in their glare
Beauty obsessed just waiting out there

Bald-headed women
But not in the UK
No you just spent hundreds today
Armed with a hair brush and spray

Bald-headed women
Don't you feel the slightest tension
As you put in your extension

I thought I'd just write and mention
Go to India, the south
Gasping with your hand to your mouth
Look at these bald headed women

You don't see that while your dancing and spinning
The man with the scissors is grinning
Not repenting for the sinning

Hair stolen like the Great Train Robbery
And it bothers me
Maybe you should be arrested for handling
But whilst you're sipping wine with your hair extensions tangling
Too obsessed about the hair that you're handling
Louis Vuitton
Handbag swings

Your favourite puppet singer sings
To lyrics they never wrote as the beat rings

Bright lights from the Taser
Live just like Fantasia
But whilst you do
Just remember those bald women in Asia.

## Licence to Kill

I need a licence to view this box
A licence to be brainwashed
Injecting my mind like a liquid cosh
Violent videos and twisted yobs

Adverts pushing
Like a bully in a playground
Making me spend my pennies and pounds
I see Iraqis screaming
In dusty, dirty lanes
Makes me believe they're not worthy
And I don't feel their pain

I wonder what would happen
If the cameras went deeper
Showed us Iraq's beauty
And not the grim reaper

Information pumped like sewage
And you are the receiver
It's up to you whether you want to become a believer

Every presenter is picture perfect
Making us feel ugly and not worth it
Look in the mirror hurting in life
Bank loan to go under the knife
New silicone implants for your wife

No that wasn't a perv grabbing fake breasts
It was a bailiff trying to claim back unpaid cheques
Insecurities landing you in great debt

Who's to blame you or me
Digital or Sky TV
Pumping information daily
Sending a generation crazy
Music videos promoting sex
Releasing their damaging hex

We look up to singers
Who get Number Ones
In videos showing off their chests and bums
All of a sudden we have a generation of teen mums

Television imprisoned
My mind
Made me visualise crimes
Music stars
Made me buy out the bar
Videos made me buy a flash car

Changing mind states just like a pill
Making a nation hate mentally-ill
Do we buy a TV licence to thrill
No it's more like 007
A licence to
Kill.

## One Life

Is it isolation from the middle-classes
That have us blinded needing glasses

Education is the path to success
See a brighter life through clean specs

The media controls the world, leaving us blind
Plays tricks with the mind
Most like a ghost won't see the signs

We're going crazy for a baby called George
But what about the child that is poor

Or the many children savaged through war?
Charities playing with your consciences
Handing over our pennies to these monsters
Or the middle-man mobsters
Does the money reach the needy or stay in their hands?
Leaving many jobless

You see we can do anything
But we are sleep-walking
Throw water in your face
Listen up when I'm talking!

One life, one life
You better leave your mark
Get up off your arse and step out of the dark
Is this really it?
Is this just a journey
I'm walking in the light
So the system can't burn me!

## It's Gonna Get Dark

I could bring about a revolution
I could create an army
But the media will make me look barmy
Undercover agents would harm me
Invisible spies would disarm me

I could turn every street kid into a militant
Tell him, stop killing him
Look in the mirror that's you kid
So killing that reflection is stupid

So we hit the streets and riot
For a few days the police turn silent
Then the media labels us violent

I could sing about freedom smoking a reefer
And like Marley get cancer or have a seizure
Maybe I could jump on the mike
Start screaming about a conspiracy
And say what I like
Screaming when thugs cry
Then like 2pac get shot in a drive-by

See, I'm sitting hear just imagining
Wondering if this was happening
Imagining like John Lennon
But I don't wanna get shot in my melon
Or like Mandela be locked-up like a felon

I can scream 'God Save the Queen'
(Is she a human being?)
And that the system is a Fascist regime
That there is no American Dream
That there's no United Kingdom
Because nobody's united
It's all bickering and fighting

Look to the skies and see
If we ain't killing you and me
Nature is coming for us

This poem does not have a chorus
Feel the horns of this Taurus
Tsunamis and twisters
Feel the mental blisters
Better protect your brothers and sisters
Animals fleeing like it's Noah's Ark
Close your eyes it's gonna get dark.

## Spilling

Kids rioting inside their brain
One day anger will explode
Then the streets will get slain

Mark Duggan shot
Then that day came

All the advertising played its part
Plus music videos topping charts
Kids running off with TVs in shopping carts
Watch the finger-pointing start

JD Sports we're coming for your trainers
We're straight up looters
We're not campaigners
Maybe entertainers

As the BBC aim cameras
Same old talk from Cameron
Kids running from batons like a Marathon

While half of Clapham raised their brooms
Kids on the Winstanley Estate sat in doom
Let's call these kids criminals
Let's not give them guidance
Now look at your streets rife with violence

But the Big Wigs sitting around the table
Are simply not able
To feel what the poor feel daily
'Cause whilst a mother struggles to feed her baby
They are chauffeur driven, lazy

Their bellies get big like oil tankers
Or those spoiled bankers
Luxury trips to Sri Lanka

Or the Indian Ocean
The poor save up *Sun* tokens
For a budget trip to Camber Sands
Whilst they will never know grands

But you will know millions
Lock yourself in your mansions
While the blood keeps spilling.

## Slave Ship Mentality

Around my town they call cars *whips*
*Necklaces* are chains
What has happened to your brains?

We commit crimes in the hope of
Becoming rich
When we're locked in chains we scream 'Life is a bitch!'

We grew up with no fathers
They were the runaway chaps
So we looked to music
To men that rapped

The nineties were the years of the brainwash
Grew up around the trains, lost
Rappers taught me that crime was clever, and spraying a gun was fun

Since I watched that rap channel the madness begun
Through my teens my sadness shun
You could look into my eyes and see levels of pain
Rap music bred the devil in my brain

They brandished guns for glamour
Now so many sons are locked in the slammer

They treated women like dirt
Now they all wear short skirts

They got paid for this
As we ran the streets trying to get rich

Where are you rappers now?
Where are you?
You see I was a kid and you had
Me fooled
Because in reality you were the fools

There's no glamour in tools
Just like no glamour in jewels

So keep your chains and whips
You're just slaves
Still locked in a ship
Chained and being whipped

You're just a puppet
A circus act
Your lyrics had such a negative impact

Now we have a generation of youths
Who are rapping too
Trying to live out this fantasy
But it's just bad news

When you promote gun shootings
You're just polluting youth
That's why we have a lost generation
Yeah that's the truth.

## Surviving on Love

Social housing, signing on the dole
Trainers swinging from a telephone pole
Burnt out cars, metal bars over windows
Dead friends blowing in the wind's flow

On the other side of town
Diamond rings glow
Fur coats and caviar
But on my side kids are stabbing ya
If you don't fit in their grabbing ya
Tears are flowing
Running not knowing
Where the hell I am going?
Sun shines over there
But over here it's snowing

Mother and father just dossed
I swear I'll make it out of here at any cost
I try to warm my hands in this frost

Now I'm walking with my hood up
Not because I don't give a fuck
But because I find it hard to communicate
Within my local streets that are filled with hate

Just like that lady wearing shades in the rain
Look around we're all hiding from London's pain

Whilst Boris and the boys sip on tea
We sip whisky and cheap beer
But one thing I have learned out here
One thing I can see clear
We better hold close
The ones we love dear

My friends seem to be falling like leaves
It breaks my heart
Watching people grieve
But I must march forward and believe

Believe in what?
Believe in humanity
Because after all is said and done
In this life
All we need is love to survive.

A DIFFERENT ENERGY

## Echoes

Sitting here reminiscing
Wishing on a star
Way up

Afar
Wishing I could do a Tracy Chapman
Fast car
Foot on the pedal
I'm young again
With my teenage friends

Before the Devil became corrupt
On a level not stuck
In this manor full of ghosts and ghouls
And twisted fools
I feel the spirits of my friends
Watching me, clocking me
Stopping me from falling
Can you two hear me calling?

The end of that youthful chapter
When a chapter ends

Right now life has got twisted
Haunted by death's kisses
Can you hear my wishes?

Another one starts
Joe
Jamaine
You are in my heart.

I walked down our graffiti-battered alley
Battered with paint and ink
Tell me what you think

'Cause I heard your echo, yeah I felt you there
I could feel your presence, I felt your stare

I closed my eyes and was running with you
Brothers of the streets
Both my friends
Wild until the end

## Stranger of Truth

We all go through spells
And experiences
We all feel different things
We all breathe the same air
We are strangers
But we are the same
We seem distant
But we are all close

You see we're not thinking the same
Are we alien?
Are we intruding?
I don't know how you feel
I judge and you do too

I think I know you
But many are playing cards that they will never show

You see you are my neighbour
But there are never any smiles

You see if you needed help
If you cried out in pain
Who would really come running?

Sometimes strangers become friends
Sometimes there was no 'strange' within the word
Sometimes we look at ourselves through the eyes of the people who don't like us

My mind is my world
Your mind is yours
You could be the man opposite
Or the lady to the left

You are only a stranger
Because there is such a word

That sounds strange

But that is so true!

## Call the Search Off

We are just searching
For answers
Not knowing
Where this path is going

We are just searching
Sometimes we seem content
Through another man's eyes
But some are hell bent

We are just searching
For things we don't need
We see and start diverting
Reversing
Asking ourselves why we were searching

Sometimes searching becomes a tough journey
Times become rough and murky
Blizzard ahead, eyesight becomes blurry
The bridge is swaying, far from sturdy

I guess from birth we are all searchers
Born to become learners
Some never learn from mistakes
Falling from grace
Falling and melting like snowflakes
Some bump their head
And spiritually awake

Searching for what?
For happiness, for peace
For a next energy like those from trees
For comfort and warmth like the feeling of fleece

Sometimes we search for
A life we already have behind our own door

Sometimes we don't need to search
We have happiness but we're stuck in hurt

Sometimes we just need to appreciate
Searching's over
So you can close that gate!

## Born to Survive

Born to survive
To stay alive on this planet
Armoured up like cash in transit
Hard as nails but I never planned it

Wherever I lay my head is my home
But I hardly sleep on the streets that I roam
Born to survive
Now what does that mean?
Middle-fingers up to post-traumatic stress
And all the shit that I've seen
Through a deathly path as a teen

Yeah 'cause I was born to survive
Now life don't faze me
Born to survive
Does that make me crazy?

Call me the urban Bear Grylls
Like I'm ex-SAS
Throw me in the deep end
Bet I'll get out of this mess
See it's all a big test

But I was born to survive
If you look deep in these eyes
You may see I've been there
But I'm still alive!

## Ego

Egos kill their own

Have you holding grudges not letting go
Just walk away
Tiptoe in silence
To a brighter day

But ego won't let you
If friends see you run
I bet you
They will laugh and tease
And that will upset you
The same friends watch you go to jail
Then forget you

Egos make you buy nice things
Gold chains and platinum rings
Ask yourself who are you impressing

You see
A man told me

He spent money he never had
Which would make him feel real bad

Bought things to keep him smiling
To impress people who didn't like him

Plus he never liked them
To the point he wanted to fight them

His ego was haunting
Had him in designer clothes, flaunting

Attracting gold-diggers
Having to peel them off like stickers
Until he focused in clean mirrors
Washed away his ego in the river

Are egos linked to insecurity?
I don't know, so you tell me
Do they fade out with maturity?
Are egos picked up
     as part of human purity?

Is this really me talking?
Walking through these words with you?
Or is it really my ego?
Let's keep walking and see where we go.

## The Gates

Standing at these front gates
Just wish they would open
Hear those creaky gates greet me

I'd walk straight through them
My whole aura will change when I spot you
Shivers come over me 'cause I love you
What are those shivers really
It feels like electricity
Like a different kind of energy
Is it my friends' spirits running through me
Running like the purest water

Pick up a pebble at random
Go with your instinct
Throw that pebble in the water

Two worlds collided
Or two hearts combined

Just standing at these front gates
When will they open?
I'm standing here and I'm hoping

I wish I was the man who never asked why
Wish I was meditating
'Cause a million thoughts and I'm aching

I don't know all of you people
What food you eat
What beat you flow to

I see your mask
And you see mine too
My electricity doesn't flow with you

I look in the mirror
And I am framed
That means my mind and body are not the same

It's like I'm standing here and my thoughts have awoken
Though we never talked
Vital words were spoken
It's time to go now the gates are open.

## Book of Faces

It's a book full of faces
Many I don't wish to see

Turn pages and feel different weathers
It's like opening up a door
Letting a hundred people walk right in

I'm not a therapist
Nor an ear to confide in
Your thoughts and feelings digging at me
This is a book I don't wish to read

Do you know my face?
Do I know yours?

Sometimes you're like a gossip magazine
Yeah that's what they should call you

You're like a nuisance caller
I can count my friends on one hand

But can you?

## Trust

So much distrust amongst us
Her scent is of beauty
Every eye follows
Complaining about the opposite sex
They are all bad
So you will attract it

Some people don't see it
Just read it and implant it
They play us off against each other
Like there is no unity

Footballers cheating on their wives
Would you have a last one night stand?
What happened to loyalty?
The grass isn't greener on the other side
He cheated
She cheated
Never seen each other again

But it's time for revenge
Then the next in line suffers the skeletons of the past

Don't let the past rattle your bones
Rattle your home

Harmony now what has happened to that?
Mother, father, child
Or children
Laughter smiles
As the camera flashes

Memories deep in the heart
Let it go
Have a little trust

Because if you close up
You will never know love

Love feels greater then hate
It's stronger
It's deeper

Tacky TV
Breeding negativity and jealousy

You see I want to be me
Not some sort of celebrity

Because I don't idolise
Like who has the X-Factor
Or who has the sex-factor

I'm not a puppet on a string
Nor holding on to those days

Let it go
Just let it go

And Trust.

## Sometimes

Feathers falling from the skies

Thought I saw your face within the crowds
Shivers causing goose bumps

Flashbacks of good times
Sometimes, sometimes

Visited the road where you lived
Just the other day

Walked the streets that we roamed as children
Stood on the steps where we sat and talked

Sometimes, sometimes
Spoke with your mother and your father too

Read a letter you sent me when you were young
Woke up in the middle of a rainy night
Question whether it was true

Sometimes, sometimes
I think about you.

**Power of Now**

Bus brakes screeching
Disturbing the peace
Red brick walls shaking
Drains rattling
That's where the rats swim

All the birds have migrated
Chewing-gum covering pavements
Pit bull crosses barking
Burly-boned men loan-sharking

Tennents get backed by the gallon
Like it's going out of fashion
Betting offices
Making you cough up your wages
Turn *The Sun's* pages
All the negativity breaks you in stages

Traffic lights on timers
Growling out the window like tigers
Anger infesting
And we still pay for congestion

We're meant to walk, greet and smile
But we acted defeated and vile
While others sail the Nile
Or travel the globe
They have us living like a roach

Sometimes these streets seem mean to me
So I jump on the train to visit greenery
I sit with my bulldog and close my eyes
I lose psychical like I'm in the sky's
Breathing fresh air
Thinking nice thoughts
For a moment with no care
Just in tune with the source

The law of attraction
Will help you escape
Make you look at the world
Make you feel great

Just a few words to make you know how
There is nothing more achieving than the
    power of now!

## A True Champ

I wonder how boxers do it
For weeks they will train
To feel punches rattling the brain
I guess that is insane

I wasn't Rocky nor Ali
But I was militant like the army
I wasn't Tyson or Lewis
But I threw my fists up to do this

I wasn't much of a pro-fighter
Never knew I would be a writer
Never new I'd be published
Though I knew I was a survivor

See champions still take beatings
Learn what it feels like to be defeated
Most become fighters due to being mistreated
Guess I became one as a street kid

I got hit with bricks and hammers too
Scars across the face
That's what slammers do

When those hits are ferocious
You see flashes and lose focus
You cover your head because the battle seems hopeless

You wear bruises and black eyes
You wear many black ties
In a world of violence and black lies

Little white lies
Get crushed in a fight, I
Have faced many demons
On this destructive path dreaming

And although I want peace
I still wake up screaming

You see a boxer bruises outside
But what really hurts is one's pride
You can't show what you really feel inside
I may of spat blood
May of screamed at Hell
I may of cut many men
I may of been cut by them

But when the bell rings out
I have to ask what I am about
When I can forgive and forget
That's when I'll stamp
A man of peace makes a true champ.

## Touching Souls

Wolves circling
A soul cowering
A heart beating
A heart bleeding

I looked on and they saw me standing
I heard them talk, knew what they were planning

The field was damp
The fog was low

If they looked closer they would have seen me glow
My hand went through them
Destiny had struck

Bodies were imprisoned
Minds dared to wander

I've seen it all
The good, the bad the ugly

Though dirty through your memories
I'm pure as could be

Traffic lights turn red
Life stops

They turn green
Life goes on

Like a forensic scientist
My words leave clues

You see I never tasted pain for nothing
Always knew I'd be something

Success is a state of mind
Balancing like a dare devil

Taking risks to achieve my goals
One day my words will touch many souls!

## Common Fate

Anger attracts anger
Love attracts love

Are we creators of our own destiny?
Am I to blame
For the consequences that I felt
For the cards that I was dealt?

Forgiveness is the key
The key to the prison door

It opens and you walk no longer in chains
But you have chains in your mind

You are keeping yourself trapped

Only the strong survive
Only the strong survive

Education is a must
It's the key to survival
Survival
Were we born to survive?
Or is that just my community?

Money doesn't buy happiness
But it can buy things
That bring happy memories

Is it all an illusion?
Do religions just divide?
Was we ever as one?
If we was one
There would be no pain

But we've come too far
We have two things in common
We breathe the same air
And one day our current consciousness will disappear
Yes it will disappear!


## Life's Bridge

Your world is within your mind
Other people won't read your signs

No one can feel another's pain
Emotions may be wild,
But expressions look plain
You cannot reach your platform
On this runaway train

If some of you only knew just to let it go
To let it go means to be free

Maybe not in body
But in mentality.

Sometimes I just stand on this bridge
The Bridge of Life we are trying to cross
Trying to reach the other side we become lost
Lost and some never become found at any cost

Sometimes the cost is to high
Trying to survive under the London sky
Guess that is why the kids get high
Asking for God with no reply

Others get lost in material possessions
This is my 'Confessions of a Street Kid'
Who rose like a Phoenix
Even when I looked defeated

Mistreated but the lesson I learnt was forgiveness
Anger consumes your soul
Keeps you locked in a dark hole

# LOCK DOWN

## I'm a Young Offender

The gate slams shut
This place is alien to me
It is scary to me
I want my mother, I want to be in my family home

I'm a young offender
They take my clothes
They take my dignity
I'm preyed on by the more hardened
They smell my fear

I'm a young offender
Surrounded by steel
The jangling of keys
The crazy noises in the dead of night
This will stay with me for a lifetime
It's damaging me

I'm a young offender
I've started to hurt myself
I put a blade to my arms
Somehow it calms me
I mean every adult I ever knew harmed me
I don't trust those officers
They lock me up and say bad things

I'm a young offender
This ain't no place for kids
Regardless of what I did
Man this place is fucking shit
I've had enough of writing about it
I swear I'll smash up this cell
I'll smash it to bits
Yeah that's for all you did
Did to me as a small kid

I went from the nervous new boy, to the
    one not to mess with

Now my fists are bleeding and my
    wounds are tender
I came in a lost boy
But now I'm a young offender.

## Mirror Kids (or Little Man I)

Little Timmy is 14-years-old
Going on thirty
From a rundown crime ridden estate, dirty

Daddy was a thief, a life of cheating
Mummies damaged from all of the beatings
Daddy's now a lifer
Timmy's now a knifer

Grey clouds over London
Shop gets robbed, keeper gets bludgeoned
These high rises are like dungeons

Crack addicts and demons
There's no sleeping through the screaming
Neighbours look through curtains dreaming

Timmy's mother's now a junkie
No school bag he's bunking

The local block becomes home
Where Timmy and his friends roam
Futures looking bleaker
As lives become cheaper

Is it their postcode?
Like a devil snatching their soul
'Cause now protecting their blocks
Have become their main goal

Fighting for social housing turf
Boris Johnson what's your city really worth?

Forget Timmy

Little Jimmy lives on the other side of town

Like Timmy he himself walks with a frown
Jimmy's mother spends her time injecting the golden brown
Jimmy's dad is also locked down

This is a lost generation
A cycle of doom
South London estates locked in gloom
What does it feel like waking up in a tomb?

Listen don't walk within Timmy's turf
You'll wish you'd never had a birth
Seems Jimmy is corrupted with the same curse
So one day Jimmy's hungry goes in search
Beyond his streets to snatch a purse

Jimmy knew the rules
Don't walk on the other side without being tooled

Jimmy looks in the mirror and thinks 'I wasn't armed'
He's woken up when stabbed in the arms
You see it wasn't a mirror in front of little Jim, no it was Tim
Ready to end him for committing the ultimate sin
That being travelling to a postcode he wasn't welcome in

The knife blade shines in the night
As it penetrates Jimmy can no longer fight
His 14 years fitting on cold concrete
Three weeks later flowers are laid at his feet

Timmy got caught and turned crazy
When he received life at the Old Bailey

So tell me why are kids killing kids and babies having babies
It's like a disease on our streets spreading like rabies
Please listen up kid
Stop dying for postcodes

Yeah I've been there

I know the roads are cold
But you're just killing yourself in reality
This gangster life is just a fallacy

Nothing's fancy about carrying a knife
Like nothing's fancy about serving life
So next time you see one of your rivals
Just remember that kid is you, stuck in survival.

## Robbers and Killers

I never had a father figure
An idol
No one to turn to when I was suicidal

Having no role model never bothered me
I just looked up to people doing armed robberies

The evil people I ran with were satanic
Needed to get a grip

I watched as they worshipped Hell
Whilst I landed in an adult jail

A man who killed another and cooked his arm
Taught me better ways to self-harm
I was 18 Killer 29
Screws thought that was fine

We would speak on the low
He would tell me disturbed info

When screws passed we would sush
He would tell me how he threw his victim's head in a bush

Those times were raw
Late at night we plotted war

He told me all about what he was in for

Taking mad pills
Felt like I was cruising
Pretending to be mentally-ill to be put into an institution

I soon got moved
With a few more loose screws in my head
I saw Killer on the news, he'll be in prison until he's dead

I cannot say his name
But he lost the first time
He played the killing game
It's mad
I looked up to robbers and killers
Like they were brothers and dads
They had guns and wore a balaclava
They showed me more love then my blood father

People wonder why I do the things I do
See what I saw you'd be a bit disturbed to!

## Moving Tomb

The moving tomb that most just pass
Eyes looking through the one way glass
From criminal courts and back to jails

There are desperate men locked in these moving cells
Some call it the 'sweat box'

Over the slightest bump your head rocks
But the hurt really comes from inside
Knowing that your bail was denied
This is when regret starts eating at lives

As you stare through the window watching the world go by
You see fathers and sons in their daily routine

You wish you could escape with the skills of a marine
But there is no escape stuck between
Reinforced steel and heavy duty door
Adrenalin pumping, sweat dripping to the floor

Watching your freedom being sucked from beneath
The prison gates on the horizon
Better grit those teeth

You wish you had been a normal citizen
Now you're locked in a box facing discipline

This box has witnessed the cries of souls
So has the warden as he patrols

Listen up Con

'Don't look through that glass          When you look out that window
Your freedom's gone                     You better repent for your sins
You're on your arse                      Hope one day a better life begins!'
Let this be a lesson to keep within

## Baby Boy

A mother's looking through the curtains
Hurting at her sons deserting

Lying to herself believing
That her son hasn't hit the road
Thieving and deceiving

Is it a mother's pride
That makes her lie inside?

Nine months in her womb
It's like her son
Wants to jump in a tomb
Enter a tunnel of doom

Her baby boy once full of joy
Brainwashed by the concrete curbs
All this worry is testing her nerves
Leaving her slightly disturbed

The son she can no longer touch
With his hood up
She loves him so much

All of the prayers ain't coming true
Police knocking on her door
Now he's running from you

He used to play on slides and swings
Lost in his eyes, his fists he swings

Singing the Jailhouse Blues
He's bad news
Mother's worst fears came true

Baby boy is a robber and a thug too

The sort that wouldn't think twice about
    mugging you

It's mental how the streets snatch sons
Is it the masses dreaming of living in
    mansions?
But most just end up behind lock and key
Raging that life is a mockery

Deep down
He's angry
The world he'll destroy
But in his mother's eyes
He's still her baby boy.

## Slammer Life

Corrupted by this gangster illusion
Has got you speaking slang in confusion
Staring in the mirror with an
Aggressive look
The path you're choosing is a depressing
    book
Better change that next chapter
Or find a pastor
'Cause on this path you capture
Demons screaming
Leaning back full of ego-swagger
Inside your clothing hides an evil
Dagger
A needle for piercing hearts

This journey is the start of
Something you'll regret

I'll put gold on it, but never bet
Gambling is like playing with flames
When you're an adult who do you blame?
We all have chances, all the same

You see your mentality attracts
Corrupted fools and rats
That's, fake women and cats
The hazards of this trap

Jury smiling, judge smashing the hammer
Flashy jewels and glamour
Leads to fools
Destined for the slammer!

## Up and Down

Razor-wire fences
Desperate men with big sentences
Robbers and killers
Shaking the premises

Now let's go back a number of years
To a little kid running with tears
Gritted teeth becoming like his peers

Clenched fist on misty days
His brothers and cousins stuck in this craze
No-one showed him another way
It was hood up and rob for his pay

He was destined to be a young offender
Mercy was for the week
So no surrender
The colder olders would sniff out a
    pretender
The role of boss was for the taking
And he was a contender

Earning stripes came naturally
He carried out robberies with accuracy
Money grows on trees
He was up to his knees deep
Night clubs and crime
Only the weak sleep

Addicted to the fast life
Like a junkie to smack
No time to relax being one of the chaps
Crazy days yeah they're loco
Undercover police taking photos
Arrested, caged up solo

You see a fast life
Is a harsh life
It will build you up
Then throw you down
Knock you from your throne
Snatch your crown

It's all well being feared
But in handcuffs you're a clown
Who's really gonna save you?
Most probably you'll drown.

## Help Me Please

Let me tell you a story about HMP
That's short for Her Majesty's Prison

But listen
Some call it Her Majesty's Poison
Because once they enter it destroys them

Some go in a Happy Merry Person
Then they start to worsen

They start going backwards not smiling
Declining, Physically, Mentally, Healthily

If you don't believe me just go and see
That's where I got my Hell Made Poetry

I would self-harm
Hurt Me Please

Don't lie to me
Doesn't matter what you're in for
Hijackings, Muggings, Piracy

All the time thinking and waiting
Is enough to make you a Healthcare
    Mental Patient

Those fours walls and bars will make you ill
In Highdown, Moorland, Pentonville
It's enough to make you squeal

Sometimes I think the system needs to
    review HMP
So many prisoners screaming for a bit of
    therapy

Look in their eyes it says
Help Me Please.

## Prison Clips

Walking the passage like
*Cool Hand Luke*
Enough jail time will make you puke
Dreaming of that
*Great Escape*
Over the wall of Whitemoor
Like the IRA
Sitting in your cell all day
Dreaming, thinking of redemption
Like Morgan Freeman
Wishing you was a free man
Ripping bars off like a he-man

Late at night you start to dig
Off to Brazil like Ronnie Biggs

Counting off the years five, six, seven
There's a Riot on Cell Block 11

The *Scum* in here will have you wincing
Armed up like a young Ray Winston

Many hours to think and smile
Wishing you had magical powers
Like in *The Green Mile*

So let's hope the
*Midnight Express*
Don't crash
And thank God they closed down *Alcatraz.*

## Little Man II

Little Timmy's grown up slightly
Years of jail got his frame looking mighty
Press ups, pull ups
This prison life is fucked up

Lonely years resting on his bed
Wrestling with demons in his head

Tossing and turning in his sleep
Screaming why is life so deep
Ghosts of his past
Tearing at the prison blanket after dark
Visions of Jimmy dying
Has Timmy waking up crying

Jimmy's coming for you Tim
Haunting you for killing him
Better ask forgiveness for your sins

Now Timmy's walking the corridors looking gory
With a face full of war stories

With nothing to win and nothing to lose
Other inmates are scared, so hide from his view

Yeah that Timmy's a lifer
Don't go near him he's a real knifer
Has no mother has no father
Daddy's gone loopy locked up in Rampton
In a drug craze held another man ransom

Mummy is fading
Years of heroin has her ageing
Five kids and they're all raging

Timmy doesn't know his brothers
No contact with his mother

At night he ties his laces around his neck
Fuck everyone and to Hell with his rep
Crying for forgiveness asking what's next

But God isn't present within these walls of Hell
Yeah it's dark within these British jails
Timmy doesn't have the guts
All this jail time is sending him nuts

Screaming out to Jimmy
Blaming him
Blaming anyone for his actions but little Tim

Uncontrollable anger
Throw the anchor to steady the ship
But Timmy's lost it
Can't handle it
Like a vandal with brick

He's smashing cells and climbing roofs
The screws have had enough and that's the truth
Shipped to the healthcare block
Liquid cosh
Time seems to stop

Drugged up on the anti-psycho medication
Has him gaining weight with his heart racing
Dribbling with the rest of the loons
Giggling like he was watching cartoons

Timmy who are you?
Who are you?

I scarred you
I scarred you

Take my hand Timmy
Look it's me little Jimmy
Yeah take my hand friend
Lets start all again

Lets escape from these blocks
Lets make a new journey
There are the knife wounds
Yeah they still burn me

Don't put your fists up
This isn't the streets
You're my brother now
And we're both at peace!

## Youngers

They went to universities
We went to Feltham
Facing uncertainties

Flashbacks attack on every anniversary
They call it rehabilitation
But it worsened me
Hardened my energy
Placed a curse on me

It's all an act
Another persona
Locked in a concrete tomb like a loner
Kids need guidance
Love and support
But they're left to perish in that court
I didn't know the reasons for my crimes
It's like I was being sentenced for treason
Time after time.

We stuck our posters up with toothpaste
Evil eyes to never lose face
I'm bruised from this place

I'm now a target
Many cards dealt
But this is the hardest
I want to wire up the door and blast it
Clean off the hinges
Crazy days
Living on the fringes

Tattooing my flesh
Screaming 'Fuck the system!'
Making friends inside
While outside I don't miss them

They call us young offenders
I call us young pretenders
I call us messed up youngers
Full of anger and hunger

Say 'Hello' to him next door
Guarantee you'll meet again
On your next tour
Whether in Wandsworth or Dartmoor
It's a long road
That's for sure!

## If that Match Don't Strike

Ten cigarettes and a box of matches
Ten bullets and a gun wrapped in plastic

Matches rattling in trouser pockets
Load up the gun and cock it

Cigarette in hand touching lips
Gun in hand with a tight grip

Match in hand trying to strike it
Enemy's house is near
Just trying to find it
Like a cancer patient wishing they could
    rewind it
When the gun sees the target
He will blind it

Destiny in the balance
The first match won't light
A family will be broken
If the next one strikes

Like a ghost watching on
But can't intervene
Pull that trigger
Prepare for a prison regime

Now you're in a cell with a cigarette in
    your mouth
You're looking for your light but it's not
    in your pouch

If roles could rotate
And time could rewind
You would of just smoked a cigarette
And not another man's mind

Like smoke bringing cancer to lungs
It's like putting a gun to your head
And taking a plunge.

## Too Short

First it was some local talk
But then it became the norm

Addicted to jail is like walking the storm
In out
Shake it all about

Walk through those gates and get the
    shake down
Strip-searched for that parcel
Shining a torch on your arsehole

Yeah it's degrading
Surrounded by the shady
Thieves, robbers and the crazy

Writing letters to your girlfriend
It's Hell friend

Screaming that you love her
But on the out
You pushed and shoved her

Now who's the mug though
'Cause she's sleeping with your cuz bro?
Revenge is a bitch
People hold grudges
It's like Karma for all sins
In front of these judges
Who are ready to pull the plug

Your's and the streets' marriage is busted
Screaming it's a miscarriage of justice
It burns like French mustard
Now it's roll-ups
Scabby, sponge and lumpy custard

Baby girl you know I need you
I'll send you a visiting order
I need to see you
Got your picture stuck on my cell wall
I'm sorry for being Hell's Fool

But she ain't writing back to you
It's like the fighting got sent back to you
Butterflies in the belly
But this shit will make you stronger
'Cause that girl is yours no longer

Yeah love hurts and jail does too
Complaining what that girl's done to you

Think about what you did to her
Lack of respect
Sentenced to years may help you reflect
So what's next?
So what's next?

*And the story goes on... You see I went to jail for three years and this was based on many men I came across and of course on my own experiences. The message here is don't take anything for granted. Life is too short to be hurting your girl. And definitely too short to live in a cell...*

## Breather

Being caged like an animal
Gives you time to think
Makes you realise life can disappear in a blink
Raindrops fall and people desert
My arm reaches through the bars with all my effort

Rat race goes by like someone pressed the fast forward button
A million men pass life's junction
No time to think, like knives
Life cuts them

I sit in a concrete tomb
Held hostage by my thoughts
Battling gloom
Since the day I left court
Wishing I could abort this mission

Just like a rat in a race
Cuffed in life's prison

Boss breathing down your neck
Like screws writing warnings at desks
Ten pints down your throat
To relieve this stress

I'm scrubbing landings
For £6 a week
Understanding
How I fell from my peak

It's through these hard times
We regret those bad crimes
It's times like this
That make you wish
You'd chosen another path
But you are paying for your sins
In this aftermath.

It's times like these
That make a normal man lead
Another life of blood and greed
Turn out a little something like me
When I was a violent, greedy teen
Bleeding on these streets

Someone press the STOP button
Before life cuts them
Take a look around
Get the hell up off the ground
I'm talking to you, so pick up the receiver
Sometimes you need to just STOP
And take a little breather!

# A POCKET OF POISON

## Golden Brown

Poppy plants from the Afghan boys
Dropping bombs don't help to destroy
Transformed into the evil brown
Needles help the human drown
Desperate souls vulnerable to the poison

Golden brown destined to destroy them
People selling their bodies
To corrupted men

Please do not enter this destructive den
Dealers live plush
Enjoying their Gold Rush

They call addicts fiends
Like their worthless beings
Open your eyes
Because you are not seeing

That's someone's
Sister, mother, brother, son

A deadly path
Like a bullet leaving a gun

Just remember as you sip champagne
You are contributing to the pain

Like a stone hitting water
There is a ripple effect

I hope my words will one day
    make you reflect
Ego
Self-image
Money scheme

Have you believe
You are living the dream
But your life is filth
Even bleach wouldn't clean
Out here
The rats and leeches are the meanest

Life is far from peaches and cream
A constant battle for addicts to get clean

But like a lion bringing down a bull
You keep pushing
Until
The vulnerable drool

One beautiful evening
The hurting will be free
From the selfish, evil and greedy

But until that day
Keep strong hold on

To all the sinners
You better right your
Wrongs.

## High

Ounces of crack broken down into stones
They call it white, rocks or bones
Smoke hitting your soul
Turning your body to bones
Teeth fading
Looking brown
And degrading
So you're out on the streets
On a shop-lifting spree
Ralph Lauren tops and D&G
Sold for a third of the price
Anything to hit the pipe

Don't worry
Got the dealer's number
Written in Biro
On the inside of my jumper
In the phone booth
I'll have two on two

That means two rocks of crack
And two of heroin
We'll be on these alleys
If it's sunny or snowing
Not knowing

Breathing like mist in the distance
Thieving has us in and out of prison

But it keeps us clean if only for months
This heroin has my arm in bumps
And lumps from the injecting
With normal society
I'm just not connecting

Not seen my kids for years and years
Was never there to wipe their tears

The crack and smack has wiped out
    this being
Drug-taking is all that I'm seeing

I'm a thief 'til the end so don't trust me
Life is now filthy and crusty
Has me sleepy in derelict buildings, dusty

These dealers have little kids
Delivering on cycles
It sends me shivers
Those kids will one day step up the chain
As another man smokes his life
    down the drain
A dealer jokes
Makes profit from their pain

Mr Crack Pipe I'd fight you if I could
Cut you with a knife
Hit you with wood
Mr Crack Pipe just leave me be
Your shadow is teasing me

These times are like slime, dirt and muck
I can no longer write 'cause
I'm high as fuck.

## Clear Vision

Little stones thrown deep into water
Little white stones corrupting
    their daughter
You call them addicts
We call them fiends

Does anyone call them human beings?
Addicted to self-destruction
Needing a quick hit to function
Now you're just a victim
    left at the junction

The pavement witnesses the low in life
Where desperate beings appear at night

Let's rewind the home video
See the innocence of a child

See joy in the eyes
See beautiful smiles

Does something twig inside?
Fast forward and the innocence
    has evaporated
Now you attract men filled with hatred
Finger nails scraping the pavement

Can they dent your body?
Can they chip at your spirit?
Can your heart feel pain?
Listen close and hear it

I've tip-toed those roads
I've run on them too
Through the alleys and pathways
Darkness looks for you

It found me
Grabbed me by the throat
And drowned me

Did I arise from holy water
Did I see the light
My fists were not clenched
But I was ready to fight

It's all in our consciousness
In our spirit,
Our energy
Only *you* can change your fate
But some are too blind to see it.

# FINGERPRINTS ON MY HEART

## Proud to Know You

Lost boys, just finding our way
Under the grey of this city
But not all memories from back then were gritty

When I look back I feel the summer warmth
But right now I'm feeling torn
'Cause another friend is gone

You may never know how I respected you
How you was strong and left early
From the local scene
From those streets
While they were turning mean

You found love
That's the stuff of dreams
But your's came true
And even though I was a crazy kid
I was so happy for you

We grew apart
But the year remained in my heart
I went off the rails completely
While your life looked so neat G
I was kicking cell doors hurting
Whilst you was working

And doing great things
You put a ring on your childhood sweetheart's finger
Hearing that made me smile

'Cause while
I was surrounded by snakes
And fake friends
I was pleased to see one of us make it in the end

We saw each other on a few occasions
Times had changed since chilling at the local station

It felt somewhat distant
But I appreciate how you became a Christian
You walked a righteous path
I respected how you had left the past
I came through it the hard way
Played my cards differently
I let the Devil tempt me

But I came back stronger
Was a messed-up man no longer

You read my writing and got in touch
I appreciated that so much

Was so happy your life turned to pleasant moods
It was like you were inviting me in
But I didn't want to intrude
Because you were now walking with God
It's like I felt rude
Or not worthy

So once again we went separate ways
Then I got that sad news on the day

The day you took your own life
Felt much worse
Than being stabbed with a knife
Just couldn't understand the strife
You clearly felt
Wonder what early cards you were dealt
That you never got over

So many questions and regrets
Like if I was there for you I bet
I could of given some advice
Now my heart feels sliced

I could never understand
How your family feel
I just pray they can deal with the pain
The situation is such a shame

Such a big loss
Since you left I've learnt much more of the man you became
Wherever you are
Here, there or way up far
I'll picture your face
When I look to the stars

I am proud that I knew you in whatever year
For you my friend I shed a tear

My memories of us as youths will play in my mind
One day I wish to find
The answers why
You and Joe left without saying 'Bye!'.

## I Will Never Forget

Have I drunk myself half to death?
Have I taken some mind-altering drugs?
Have I learned to use a part of my brain
Turned off by this world?
I see you standing
I reach out to hold you
I fall straight through you
I graze my head, but feel no pain
I hear you, I can smell you
Is this a vision?
Is this a dream?
Don't you just leave?
Don't you just go?
Did you ever watch over
See the tears that fell?
Did you reach out?
Was you that shiver that came over me?
Was you that small feather that landed?
Are you proud of who I've become?
Do you wish you was still with me?
Have you walked beside me
    on this journey?
I just want you to know
I feel your presence
I know it's real
The presence of my past friends don't
    haunt me
Is this a gift?
Or just my imagination?
I feel comfort
I feel joy
I just want you to remember
That I will always remember
That I will never forget
Yes, I will never forget!

## Limey

We nicknamed him Limey
Breath stinking of spirits
Old, dusty and grimy

Had walked off-course on life's journey
I sipped on spirits too
And they would burn me

The local tube station
Got a rude awakening
When we started congregating

Me and my friends spent time
At the end of the Northern Line
Security shared with London's drifters
Sore like blisters
Caught up in this city's twister
Did I hear Limey's whisper

Somewhere down this street of cobble
Limey's life wobbled
Swayed and dropped
Found himself like me propped up
At the station
Facing
Alienation
Concrete grounds pacing

For a dare I passed him a beer
His alcohol addiction was clear
He thanked me but then left in fear

Fear of being attacked
Fear of kindness
Was I guilty of a dare?
But I no longer cared

I made a man in despair
Smile if only for a while

Wake me up on this journey
Those brown spirits burned me
Gave me ulcers in my tummy
I was a child
Should have been with my mummy

But I was on London's cold roads
Lost and grimy
With the walking dead
Men like Limey

In and out of prison
Anxiety held me in this position
The station never saw me for a while
Limey forever asked after that lost child
That child was me
Probably the only friend he had

Where's my friend he would cry
I was crying too
Locked in a concrete tomb

Now Limey's long dead
Brown bread
Reminiscing on the time we spent

Once they were called
Gentlemen of the road
Now they're tramps and lost souls
With a bag attached to a stick
They would stroll
Now it's a bottle of alcohol
An unfair burial like that of a slave
Did they throw a rose
    on your pauper's grave

Limey, though grimy
Was a man so brave
Would cause havoc on the streets
Just vanished without a trace

Wherever you are my friend
I hope you're in a better place.

## Chantel

Whatever happened to Chantel
Whatever happened to you?

Running from your ghosts
Dodging the inspector
Looking over your shoulder
Crossing anyone
That stepped in your path

Where are you now?
Haven't seen you for a decade
Are you locked away
Staring through bars?
Are you healthy
Or are you still scarred?

I was just a boy
Bunking-off from school
You were ten years older
Ten years wiser

We climbed through that hole
We entered that squat
You took a hot bath
Cleansing your lost soul
I was sitting with strangers
They offered me Class-A
I should of been in class that day

It was smiles all around
My school uniform stood out
I looked on and wondered
Your hands went through their money

You shared the steal
Although you crossed everyone
With me you was real

You kissed me on my lips
And I kissed back
With hindsight
I can laugh at that

Maybe you passed on your bad vibes
Your negative flow
'Cause you didn't stick around to watch
    me grow

Whatever happened to Chantel
I'll keep asking myself
Where are you now?

I'll keep asking myself
Like a butterfly lost
Not finding it's way
You disappeared that day
We were running from a shoplifting spree
And you were way ahead of me
I saw you in the crowd over at the station
I glanced again and you were not there
I could no longer see
Your ginger, curly hair
'Goodbye' Chantel wherever you are
I hope you found peace
I hope you're not scarred.

## To You

It's a winding road
With twists and turns
Emotions change
Like the season too

Whilst I try to find my way back to you
People pass and smile my way
Some stop to ask if I'm okay
Street lights flicker above my head
Above them stars start to glow

Like the river I carry my flow
I can no longer feel my feet
Can't see my shoes
Whilst I try to find my way back to you

Leaves fall from trees
Brown from the autumn breeze
This journey's tiring
And I'm down on my knees
I look to the skies and beg
Please
Does anyone hear my cries
Maybe a few

Whilst I try to find my way back to you
It's like a marathon
Feels like this will never end
Through these winding roads
I'll find my friend
I've walked these roads before
Yeah, I'm sure it's true
I adjust my eyes
Is this *déjà vu*?

I've found my way back to you

## Jamin T

Talented with lyrics
Fast or slow
Story-telling was part of your flow

You made me write this
You inspired this

A waste of talent
A waste of life
Now your people are stuck in strife

Some knew you as a Lavender Boy
Now you walk in fields of lavender

Some knew you as Jamin T
Tearing up the mic
With your ABC

Some knew you as Chez
Remember we fell out
And you made the crew Nuff Vexed

Painting panels for a living
Plus we painted train panels for kicks
Reminiscing on when we were kids

You see the pain
I felt from your parting
Had me with a pen
Starting
To write rhymes
So you inspired
*Street Crhymes*

Remember when these streets were ours
When we were close pals

Now I'm shouting 'Rest in Peace!'
Remembering
How you blessed these beats…

## The Pack

This ain't no gang it's a pack
Sandy colour, patches on the back
Koko and Buster
Like sister and brother
Red and Ted
Like bread and butter

Lock the park gate
No escaping
It's a play fight
No scraping

Others watch with Poodles and Danes
They're not part of this pack not the same
They get judged like kids and that's a shame

Loving and loyal
Digging up the garden
Noses covered in soil
Like babies get spoiled

Patches the colour of timber
Another joined the pack
And that will be Simber

Misunderstood but that's how it is
They might fight another dog
But don't bite kids

Is it the bulldog in the bloodline
'Cause it seems those dogs are doing hard time

Simber was the first to be put down for the crime

I swear Red and Bust had their own special bond
One eye off the ball
And Red was gone

What happened officer, where is my hound?
It was a danger to the public so got locked down

What, that cuddly dog that loved to play the clown?
Yes and it escaped from the police compound and was never found

Are they trying to make it back
Homeward bound?
Simber and Red they're missing now
So it's just Buster and Koko kissing now

Jack Russel barking like a beast
Now I wish Buster was tied to a leash
But it wasn't to be
Buster got hold of the dog
And made it bleed on the streets

A year we waited for him to be freed
But now he's resting in Pet Cemetery

It's testing me
As the rest of the pack get older
Now Teddy and Koko
Are looking over their shoulder.

UNCONDITIONAL

**Sweet Child of Mine**

You're like the breeze when life gets too hot
Like the calming effect of gentle Caribbean waves
Your cheeky smile
Such a delight

Sweet child of mine
Precious could not describe
Beautiful could not explain
This world does not hold the words
To let my girl know
How daddy loves her so

Sweet child of mine
To enjoy every moment of your innocence
Before you grow older
In this funny old world
Daddy's little girl
You leave fingerprints on my heart
You leave footprints through my journey

Sweet child of mine
Sweet child of mine.

## Happily Ever After

I was too scared to hold you
'Cause before you was born
I was a cold fool

Lost and wild
Looking into the eyes of my child

My tears were clean
They flowed like pure water

I only ever knew painful ones
Before having a daughter

Couldn't touch her with hands
That we're used for fighting the next man
Couldn't hold her near due to the fear of breaking
Didn't want her to feel my scars of being forsaken

The first year
I followed in my father's footsteps
Until late at night
To your cot I crept
I sat there watching
As you slept
I sat there
All night
And wept

It was time to be a man
Do the right thing
Start bringing stability to your young life
Be a good daddy day and night
I had hope and knew I had made things right

Just the two of us
Doing great things

Happy memories I'll cherish from
Within

You see when a child is born
It's like a flower growing

It's like I had love inside the whole time, just not knowing
You brought out the caring
The kindness
The sharing
My life was no longer tearing
Or ripping

I was flipping the script
Re-writing my path

Now you are five-and-a-half
Full of sweetness and laughter

I've been setting the foundations
For you to live happily ever after.

## Pillow talk

Lying with my head on this pillow
It must of heard the thoughts of a
    thousand caged men
Thoughts of rage
Thoughts of emptiness
Regrets and hopeful wishes
This pillow
This pillow

Taking gambles in life like bingo
Hear my thoughts as I tiptoe

You see I never had a pillow to share
Until I saw you standing there

My pillow was cold
Had supported lost souls

I found myself walking
The land of the lost
Even when I was free
Freedom was nothing until
    you came to me

Did you shed a tear on my pillow?
Did you share your energy?

You see since you have entered my life
My pillow feels warm
Like no more strife

Since you came in
It has stopped raining

Now I share my pillow
To share is to open-up

To put trust on the line
To lay myself bare

Leaving myself open for hurt
But with you it's pleasant times
Good vibes

Let's put our heads on my pillow
Close our eyes!

## A While Ago

It's been a while since I told you
It's been a while since I would hold you

That look in your eyes
Laughing at my humour
The next time we met couldn't come
Any sooner

So I started off a little rumour
Hoping it would get back to you
That you had me wooed
Hoping I was on the right track to you

Like a prison gate
My feelings were locked
Like a key
You opened up

Like a sprinter waiting for the sound of the gun
Like a racer reaching the final bend
Like the winning team collecting their prize

It's been a while since I looked in your eyes
It's been a while since I would hold you
It's been a while since I told you
That I love you.

## My Greatest Auntie

Born with a gift to sing to a nation
To follow your dreams you faced migration

It must of been scary at such a young age
To leave your loved ones to perform on a stage

You took the jazz scene by storm
As Lambert, Hendricks and Bavan would perform

Gifted in many ways as well as singing
Performing and acting

You had the jazz scene swinging and spinning
But most of all you are such a pleasant being

Spiritual and warming through your energy
And this carries through to your melody

You see many years I was searching
Hurting all because

I had Sri Lankan blood
But didn't know who I was

And then we reunited
In this life of mine

And I learnt so much in such little time
You made me so proud of my Sri Lankan roots

But most of all just knowing you
You're my great auntie

And Great is the right word to describe you
Now you're an inspiration
In all that I do.

## No Ordinary Love

I'm nothing without you
I'm something with you

The saying goes
'Behind every man there's a good woman'

See, I know you are good
I know you're true

If I say that I am bad
Is that my destructive side?

Will we grow old together?
Like those old folk

Hand-in-hand on the beach
Eating ice cream

Though you're not my child's mother
You love her like your own

And she loves you too
We both do

If my writing blew
If it went worldwide

Would you still be by my side?
If my story turned to film

Could I still turn to you?
You will never see me sipping bubbles

Will never see me walking with them
'Cause when all said and done
I only trust you

And my little princess
For me to trust was a barrier so high

Now I do I'll give you everything
We're deeper than the average

This is no ordinary love.

MORE TALES FROM THE DARK STREETS

## The Devil Wears Prada

Pot bellied men throwing notes
As she grinds up and down on the pole
Nice and slow
With everything on show
Designer clothes
Addicted to watching diamonds glow

This is the girl's life
Flying high like a kite
The world's at your feet now
It's millionaires that you meet now

Convertibles cruising through the night
Your hair blown in the wind
Like this is the life
Gangster by your side
Switching gears while you ride

Brother wondering what happened to his sister
How he missed her
But she's lying next to a gang-banger waiting for the whisper

Pillow talk
That's dangerous
And this slick girl is a stranger
Cocaine up the nostril
Like something from a novel

Trying to find that gold,
Hidden like a fossil
Situation will soon get hostile
Grown woman not a lost child

Evil circles
So don't cry tears when she hurts you

Sends in her boys
And deserts you

Remember, remember
Just like the fifth of November
As a spark hits the gunpowder
There will be a gun shower

This city struggles for power
Muzzled dogs
Victims cower

Her money's getting up now
So much coke
She don't give a damn now

Old Bond street
Hatton garden
Flashing cash
This girl has hardened

Catching attention
From thugs flying high
Even corrupted police
I'm *not* gonna lie

Dodgy buisnessmen
And buisness moves
Walk in her shoes
She'll have you on your ones and twos

You move smart
But she moves sharper
And she retaliates harsher
Then she's relaxing on luxury yachts in the harbour
This is the definition of the Devil Wears Prada.

### Little Gary

Little Gary became a head case
Watching his mum make the bed break
No father figure
Just pimps and dealers
With fingers on triggers

This ain't no movie
No news story

Bear with me while this tale gets gory
This is where there will be no glory
Just a bunch of men that are predatory

Like a spider catching that fly in his web
A few hours after struggling that fly's dead
Flies hover around shit
Flies hover around these pits

Lord of the Flies
Demons and ghosts
Got little Gary's mind turning gross

Cold to touch
Filthy house playing with creatures
Touched by the beast
Just look at his leaders
Cutthroats and bleeders

Black eyes and bruised back
From the smacks and the beatings to his head
That's what you get for peeing the bed

Stale bread
And lumpy mash
While the pimp smacking his mum counts up the cash

So he's climbing fields with his penknife
Fantasising about making it slice
Stuck in this hood life
Oblivious to a good life
Cutting the legs off of wood lice
Tearing them from spiders
See the fire burning in his eyes
Surrounded by liers
Duckers and divers

It leaves its wear and tear
Then he saw the neighbours' cat sitting there
That white fluffy hair
Soon turned red
His smile so wide it stretched his head
So what's next

Penknife under his brown pillow
Communicating has turned to zero
Fuck a super hero
That's just wive's tales
There's no escape when your life's hell
And the damage was done
He stabbed that man who smacked his mum
They are all to blame for this murderous son

It wasn't one stab wound
It was multiple numbers
I guess this house raised hunters
Hailstones and thunder

Young offender institution
Guess it beats prostitution
The other boys know he's cranky
Fascinated with shanking
So when they walk past him they're blanking

And his face is blank
His heart is too
Let's head to the Broadmoor zoo
Now it's goodbye to you

'Cause little Gary's become a headcase
Visions of his mum's bed shaking
His mum's bed breaking

The wheels on this car
Are scraping
Leaving tyre marks
Watch the fire sparks

Those pimps with weapons caused war
Now little Gary's sectioned in Broadmoor
Forever on a ghost tour.

## Vice System

The Devil snatched her from Albania
Men threw her around,
    like wrestling mania

Drugged into submission
Red light district
Equals human prison
She prays to God but no one listens
Pimps fist and her face
In another collision

Weed smoke fills the air
High on coke blokes stop and stare
Like a piece of meat on display
In Amsterdam
Another filthy man
His trousers down
Desperate
An addict injecting brown
Eyes closed
Clothes thrown
Cold toes
Heavy breathing
Through the nose
Don't trust the man on top
Don't trust the other whores
Day dreaming
Inside screaming
Pimp is scheming

Thoughts become sinister
Put your phone down
Don't call a solicitor

In this world
Scores get settled on the streets

A little like a butcher putting metal to meat
Murder may be the only way to end the deceit

Heavy music pumps the ground
Crazy drugged women jump around
Pimp takes his eye off business
Starts playing the clown
Takes the Albanian girl in a room
Says, 'Don't make a sound!'

You see when the Devil touches
It leaves you disabled
Needing crutches
Bleeding internally,
Your whole spirit crushes

Her eyes were black like the night
A crack running through pure white
A butterfly with torn wing
A wife crying
Throwing her ring

She's out there somewhere
But most wouldn't know
She could be doing your hair
No thought she used to be a whore

As he clambered on top
She forced the razor deep
His neck wound wept like a widow
'Cause death was in the air
As he coughed and choked
All she could do was stare

She could be the girl next door
Or just up the street
You may never know
She was hacked at like meat

You can never judge a book by the cover
See that man fucking her
Could have been your brother
A friend, work colleague or other

When she looked in his eyes
It took her back
To when she was pure
Before this demon and his lure

People play with cards and fire too
Better watch out
Or it will fire at you
Yeah that's right you will get burned
Count your blessings
Before tables turn!

Running through fields of grain
Breeze blowing away the pain
A blast from the past
She screamed in his face
As he took his last gasp
To overcome this trauma
Will be more than a task

So this is how the story ends
She took his money and ran from his gory friends

## Calm After the Storm

She had to crawl past the step-dad
Whilst the punk was past it drunk

Risk waking him and feel a punch
Or a kick in the ribs
Got me crying life's a stupid bitch
How the hell is he hitting kids

You see it's like this
Actions have consequences
Broke her teeth she got sent to the dentist
Ruining the smile of child

It's like starting a fire
Deep within
That kid grows up and the flames
    keep spreading

Wish I could of stuck my head in
With a next force
Push my mind through walls
And shout at you
Scream abuse at you

'Keep your fists to yourself
Keep your fists to yourself'

But I am just human
And that leaves me fuming
My ear to those walls trying to tune in

I never knew her
Way back when
You and your friends would abuse her

Now I'm karma and you can't harm her

I'm watching, I'm clocking
I'm outside your window plotting

Whisky hitting your liver
I was that shiver
Down your spine
I was that empty bottle of wine

A pretty girl disfigured from living
Not giving a damn
About the next man beating her
Mistreating her

See you set the foundations
This was your painful creation
Where's the explanation

Where's the apologies?
Instead you're wallowing in self-pity
'Cause you broke a child
    and made her life shitty
Last time I saw her
Years of watching my own back
Made me feel her aura

I felt her vibe
Knew the next time I saw her
She wouldn't be alive
Yeah I saw it in her eyes
Her fake smiles

Standing on that bridge
Flashbacks of a kid
They felt like the very first punch
She climbed over and jumped

Got hit, split in two by a train
Pretty girl, no more pain
No more pain

It's such a shame she wasn't stronger
Now I'm waiting outside your house no longer

Back in the draw goes my knife
'Cause in reality you're taking your own life

Just like she did
But she had excuses

While you drink yourself to death
You're useless
As a young man you were ruthless
Left a pretty child toothless

Last time I heard
Your situation was critical
Hooked up to a machine
The drink ate at your physical
Take this as my subliminal

The crows were circling at the crack of dawn
The lights turn off
That's two lives gone
This is now the calm after the storm.

### Daddy's Running

I can't get a job
I swear I'm trying so hard
Praying that my cards will change
That times will
Re-arrange
Now I have a child on the way
Another mouth to feed
That big break is all I need

Doorbell rings
I'm met by muscled men
They want to take my things
So I tussle with them
Handcuffed I'm arrested again

Six hours later I'm at my flat once more
But my pregnant girlfriend won't open the door
I lose my temper and call her a whore

I'm hurting her so I'm hurting me
All I want is to feed my family
Next I scream through the letterbox

'I'll do better, I'll do better, watch'
So I walk the streets broken inside
But to Hell with her seeing me cry

I just want that perfect home
Though I feel like I'm in the Worthless Zone
I've been clean from the drink and the Class-A
But once again I'm drinking from that glass today

This London town is getting me down
Flash cars whizzing past
Walking past posh and busy bars

That's when I pulled up this fitted scarf
To cover my face from the CCTV
I will commit a robbery like you see on TV

Adrenaline pumping
As sweat pours and my heart's jumping
But damn it I'm jumping

Over that Post Office counter
Pound sterling I want to be counting

I want a large amount
I'm climbing this mountain
Whilst crazy times are mounting
I'm falling like water from a fountain

Cash spilling out my pockets
Energy like electricity flowing through a socket
I'm running for my life now
I've thrown the knife now

Run, son, yeah I'm running for you
And if the police catch me
I'm still coming for you
My unborn son
I'll show you better than this
On your soft head I'll place a kiss

My son, my unborn son
Daddy will do better
But I'm on the run.

COLOUR BLIND

## Paki

I looked in the mirror and saw
A white kid
Never realised a flame had ignited
Ashamed of my roots
I was fighting
And at the same time frightened

Brown skin with a white family
Deep within it was testing my sanity
Fitting in was a constant fantasy

'Kick the paki's head in,' they shouted
Kicked on the floor, it's the brown kid
But one day I'll fuck up this town kid

You made me hate myself
Like cheese I would grate myself
Self-harm
Self-harm
Would keep me calm
See the razor slices up my arms

You see I never knew any other Asians
Mixed white
But never a brown relation
Wishing I could fly through the sky
Like a raven
Become a new creation
In a different location
But I was stuck in this place
And facing a battle of proportions
When I see a bully
They better approach with caution
Or face regret
Like an abortion

Pushing me again
Would be your misfortune

Crazy how the tables turn
Now let your racist labels burn
Like a man wounded but fighting-on
Through my writing read my wrongs

You see
No regrets, no regrets
Racist bullies made me
Slightly crazy
But then onto stability

You see
I was ashamed of my roots
Hated my colour
Became the craziest kid in my borough
Lost myself along the way
But when I look in the mirror today
Deep in my eyes
I see a man with respect and dignity
Honour with the ability
To help others
Sisters, brothers being bullied
Kicked to the ground
I look in the mirror and stand proud

Be yourself
Stuff being one of the crowd.

## Colour

Colours can be bright
Some can be dull
Colours can be erased

Colours can divide
Can separate
Colours can cause wars

Colours we can paint
Paint a picture
So you can't see the true colour
Is black dark and dark bad?
Is white pure and pure clean?

So what makes a mixture of
Both
Good and evil

Colour causes war
Colour causes war

Without colour art would seem plain

Funny how some colours
Wish to be darker
Some colours
Wish to be lighter
Being a certain colour could turn you
    Into a fighter

What if there was no colour?
What if the word never existed?
What if we couldn't see
Could only smell?
Would there be so much hatred
So much war?

Colour causes war
Colour causes war

Am I not welcome due to a colour?
Am I just using colour as an excuse?

Tattoos
Scars
Have dented my colour

What is the colour of your heart?
What is the colour of mine?

It's all the same colour.

## Confessions of *The Sun*

Look I'm going to read *The Sun*
Turn to page 3
And see breasts and bums

Oi mate watch your nerve
I'm just a man
I'm not a perv
Alright gorgeous let me feel your curves

You see my missus is boring
When she climbs on top
I'm snoring

And she's bored too
She's cheating with her boss Luke
I read the texts
I know it's true
But what shall I do
I guess I'll stay with her
'Cos I ain't got a clue

So I turn to page 5
Can't believe my own eyes
Bloody Muslim mum
Claiming benefits, 'What utter scum'!

My taxes are paying for this whore
Coming to my country
Running from war
I mean what fucking war
They're terrorists
That's what we were there for

I mean I'm a law-abiding citizen
Never committed a crime
Never been to prison

Always paid my way
I turn to page 6
And see a bloody gay

Fucking queer
I hope one of those types
Never comes around here
I mean, it just ain't right
How can a man be another man's wife

Listen I bloody love reading *The Sun*
Even though it tells me of scum
Black robbers on the run

So I turn to Dear Deirdre
Emotional tosh
Brings tears to me eyes

Get this
A woman wrote in grieving
Said she's leaving with her kids
Says her husband's a pervert
Always going on about tits
Doesn't make an effort
No he doesn't give a shit
Husband sounds like a right git

She says he's racist, sexist and
    homophobic too
And she's had enough
Dear Deidrie what shall she do?

She says she's packed her bags
And is leaving with Luke
Luke, fucking Luke
No this can't be true

## Angry Men

That can't be
My Brenda leaving with Luke
Is this some sick joke in *The Sun*
Is this what you do?
Messing up my mind
Filling it with dog poo
Making pervy images
Stick in my mind like glue

Well, 'To Hell with you'
Luke and her
And what you looking at you wanker
I'll throw you in the river like an anchor

Well if it's like that Brend
Have this then
Four years ago
I fucked your tutor
Well come on then

Step up to this bruiser
Agh, stuff this I'm off to the boozer!

Extremism taking over this land
I wonder if this situation was planned
Were they really al-Qaeda fanatics
Or deluded maniacs
Moving, frantic?

Now this land does look frantic
Racial issues becoming gigantic
Mosques being torched
Looks like unity will never be forged
Or we can pretend and be false

But anger and hatred will still linger
Like Triads cutting off fingers
Like the IRA blowing knee-caps
There will never be peace so we scrap
Throw fists up
Throw petrol bombs
Burning skin like metal tongs
Look around you and see it's all wrong

Look a bit deeper
See this system has us in a sleeper
It's a horror
Jeepers creepers
We're the sheep
And they are the keeper

I'd love to sit back and stare
On these so called enemies out there
On these chairs
Airing their views
Instead of throwing flares
Walking with hateful stares

Just be grateful for this land we share
Just be grateful we have food and water
That there are schools
To educate *your* daughter

Still I see EDL sprayed on walls
May my writing educate these fools
Pissed up on Stella walking with tools

But who am I?
I'm just a man with a pen
I used to be more angry than them
This is just how the anger vents

Or are we all just angry men?

## Munching History

Do schools really teach the truth
Who really plans out
The exam books

If a teacher was to disagree
What would happen to he or she?
Is their knowledge power?
I don't think so

Does this system dumb us down?
Are we taught to worship the Crown?

If you fail a few GCSEs
Only get Cs and Es
Does that mean you can't succeed?

Never
A few ticks on a sheet
Doesn't make you clever

Reading pages
Studying the world in stages
You see many don't know
Many just judge
We just push and shove
The television programming our brains
With nonsense
Playing on our subconscious

The Black Plague
The Black Death
The black market

Your words are the harshest
'Cause if black means dark and dark
    means murky

Then your dictionary hurts me

White means light
And light means brightness
Or illumination

Now you wonder why we are hated
But if I play the race card
My white friends will feel slated

See the working-classes
At civil war
Poor killing the poor
Black against white
It's all one big fight

But we have more in common
With the foreign
Than the judges and the rulers
The ones who beat us with rulers
Or canes
Like when slaves were cutting sugar
So calling them cotton pickers
Is like having no brains

Why do we call some Yanks rednecks?
'Cause they were slaves too on the decks
The masters sipped iced drinks in bed
Whilst the white slaves' necks turned red
From the sun burning
Life is about learning
Twisting and turning

Ever looked at the well-travelled
Most have dabbled in different cultures
Broken down the sculptures

That were planted in them
Becoming open-minded men

You see our western TV
Doesn't show us the pure beauty
Of some of the countries we see

It shows us blown-up buildings
Scruffy, dirty children
Making us feel that we're better
When it's us causing the mayhem

Our country is pure power
We stand proud
As individuals
Backed-down
Bowed out to the crowd

Forget those ragheads
Are they the ones creating
        our skag heads?
How the hell does it get through customs
It's strange how the cycle functions
Step back up
Prepare for the truncheons
Just remember
It's mostly bullshit were munching!

# ALL IN MY HEAD

## Lately

I've seen enough to drive a sane man crazy

I said lately
I've seen enough to drive a sane man crazy
Maybe these thoughts have been in me
    since I was a baby

Spreading through my mind like rabies
Growing in my head
Like egg to caterpillar
Was my life destined to be a thriller
From pupa to butterfly
But my life would never be smooth
Like butter
Why?

Because the only fly was the lord of them
Possessing my life like a demon
Banging my head off cell walls screaming
Wishing I'd wake up from this dreaming

But dreams were reality
Just a ghost to my family
I graduated to the nut house academy

Because lately
I've seen enough to drive a sane man crazy

Tormented from past trauma
Hell bent you could see it in my aura

We can't go on together with
    suspicious minds
So I sit in my pit
And write vicious rhymes

On how one child wrote a series
Of memoirs
Setting off alarms
Like smoke from cigars
On another planet
Strolling through Mars
Damaged from life
Feel the mental scars

I'm going to war with myself
Like soldiers in Iraq
To make sure I never fold in the dark
Because surviving my life
Is far from a walk in the park

If I buckle in this daily hustle
Doctors will arrive with needles and
    inject my muscles
Have me doped-up
Mentally roped-up
In a strip-cell
Ripping up their interior
Because they believe
They're superior
That their lives are merrier
Because I snap at them like a terrier

Because lately
I've seen enough to drive a sane man crazy.

## Sevens

My whole life is like a war, man
Like a soldier on tour, man

This post-traumatic stress
Making me act in strange ways
These are strange days

And I don't feel with it
I swear I can't deal with it

Like three soldiers fell down
It's Hell now
Those soldiers were my close friends
Asking God why he chose them

Having visions of my child
Experiencing my childhood
Going through the shit I did
It's like I sit and cry for my kid

Or am I crying for the kid I used to be
For that childhood spirit
Deep inside of me

Sevens like who the eff are you
You see boy
See what those scars do

I look in the mirror and I see you
    in my eyes
See you in my shadow
And you're making me mad bro'

See what you made me do
It's like I'm hurting me
So am I hurting you?

## Nomad

I'm causing all the heat in this kitchen
The reason for your bitching
The reason for my switching
The reason your heart's bleeding

Yeah you wasn't corrupted like me
But you liked me
And I liked you
I was on a high
Like look what I do

I should of never called you
'Cause now I've stalled you
I told you I had changed
But I fooled you
Tried to be your knight in shining armour
Tried to school you

I flew you around the world in two years
Wish you had never shed two tears
But now you shed many
Tell me is our love empty?
Is this engine running on empty
'Cause it seems like we used to
    have plenty?

I wish I could say leave
Go and never come back
But I always want you back
Like if I go back
On my nomadic journey
Would that decision burn me

I feel like saying 'Fuck it'
Grab your heart and chuck it
You don't understand me

'Cause I don't understand me

So tell me how can we be?
And that's the question

How can we be?

## Stay

Stay with me
Stay with me in insanity
Stay with me on this path of destruction
Middle-fingers up whilst we function

Stay with me forever and a day
Whilst we clash with authority
Stay with me
Don't you ever leave
You see these walls bleed
You see the leaves on these trees
Turn from green
To brown and crispy
Blowing like dust in the wind

But don't follow the wind's flow
Stay with me on this crazy road
Stay with me

They know it's doomed
But all we see is each other in the room
Should I take your hand and place a ring
Or would I die like a bee after the sting
In the afterlife you're still my queen
And I'm your king.

## Self-healing

Fear eating me since a child
Deceiving lost and wild

Looking for that father figure
At times left me rather bitter
One thing though, I was no quitter
Time moved on
It's like I lost my sister
Though I love her
I'm sure I don't miss her

I look in the eyes of my girl
Wondering how she will prevail in this world
Unconditional such a deep word
Anxiety for my child tests my nerves

I realise I'm looking at myself
I once risked it all to amass great wealth
I no longer wish to delve
Would love to be somebody else

It's all in my head
They pointed the finger and that's what they said
I look in their eyes swearing
I'll fight to the death

To feel smiles I must start to begin
To heal the child deep within.

## Searchlight

Stuck in a hole
I saw my soul wobble
Now it's like they paint me as a role model
While others wanna test my bottle

I've got my back to you
The engines at full throttle

When you've glimpsed at the gates of Hell
And flipped your life to tell

Bookworms on how you fell
Into the pit of self-destruction

Explained how your young mind functioned
How you kept your heart pumping

From a thief to receiving pats on the back
To living in the same town,
    being one of the chaps

I feel the weight on my shoulder trap
In fact
At times I feel trapped

For me it was my destiny
Went through the dark
To see the best of me

I wrote on walls,
To books to poetry
Now it's like the whole town's
Knowing me
Some hate stuck in self-pity
When they haven't lived a life
Half as gritty

Some look to me for help
Support and advice
And I find that warming
Somewhat nice

But sometimes I have to pinch my skin
'Cos it don't seem real

How can these people be coming to me
When I was so ill
Then I realise they were like me
Broken and hurting

It's like I found my way
But they've got to keep on searching.

# THE GOOD STREET

## The Struggle

I see the struggle in your eyes kid
Surrounded by the lies kid
Living up to this gangster image
It's dirty like sewer spillage
It's tough on the other side of the village

It's cold on the pavement
You have to show braveness
In many situations
It's an uphill journey you are facing

It's all a learning curve
It's all education
Punching the walls
Locked in the police station

I know you're waiting for your chance kid
You just want to glance kid
See a better life through these glasses

Mother's bills are not paid
On deadline
Living below the breadline
Got to get your head right

They say they're cutting handouts
Then they party
Get the band out
Rich get filthy
Poor stay dirty
Look down their nose
It hurts me

And I see it hurts you
'Cause I see it in your eyes kid
Surrounded by the lies kid

The media have us blinded
Like the sunshine and the paper
Paper, paper
Read all about it
The news tells the truth
I doubt it

Walk in the shop and you're followed
Swallowed by close circuit television
See I had this vision
That this world is just a prison
A prison for the poor

Who will risk their freedom
To gain more
Ten Downing Street is a prison door

Listen kid they can chain your arms
But your mind remains free
It's plain to see
Just take a look at me

I went from fighting
Swinging left hooks
To creative writing
And selling books

They can kick you when you're down
But you better get up and rise
Chin up kid
Get that struggle from your eyes!

## Narrow Roads

Violent men meet in narrow roads
Anger consumes harrowing souls
No sane man can say
That this lifestyle isn't a painful way
A painful route

Wishing that you'd picked a different fruit
Wishing you could dilute the brute
Inside
But no matter how you try
With like-minded men you collide

'Cause violent men meet in narrow roads
Anger consumes harrowing souls
It's a life of blood and guts
Of thugs and cuts

Healing wounds
You walk that street feeling doomed
The truth is sometimes you have to walk
Walk away and run if it helps
Channel your anger into something else
Your real friends would understand

You shouldn't have to prove yourself
Using and bruising your hands
And to walk away
Really does take a real man

Some have to rewrite their own fate
Before they get locked
Behind steel gates

I've seen the life I know how it goes
Everywhere you stroll
Your history will follow

And when the police again arrest
Other fighters are deemed innocent
Because they see you as the pest
They are your demons
You are the one possessed

It's 'cause violent men meet in
    narrow roads
And anger consumes harrowing souls!

## Shifting Labels

They say don't hang with the bad kids
Speak slang, smoke cancer sticks
We set fires, threw stones and bricks
Windows smashing
Adrenalin pumping
Garage roof-to-roof we were jumping

Like a child born disabled
They tagged us with labels
Which brainwashed our mental
And stuck like staples
Led us onto a path that was fatal

Adults were carers
Meant to guide us
But branded us terrors
Had us finding underground cellars
Years later, high on drugs
Flying like propellers
Some became heavy duty
Like the Goodfellas

Living a Scarface fantasy
The gang was our family
Some jumped from life's balcony
To escape this insanity

We were fallen like leaves
And that leaves
Others lost and stuck in more grief

My point of these words
Is don't label a child with words
That stick like glue
Would you like someone labelling you?

A question for you people
Are children really born evil?
You claim to be caring
But you are see-through
Your words hurt like a needle

So my aim is to be rid of them
Labels produce violent men
Look back
See that kid
Was a product of his environment
Just a small child needing guidance
Now he's grown
Lost in life
And you can't find him
You act blind
And tell yourself
Never mind him

And to you lost kids turned men
Start unwinding
Discovering and finding
The root of your madness
The root of your sadness
Remember letting go of this raft
Will free your mind from the past
Though you look to the skies
And they're overcast
This bullshit bad weather won't last

It's all a learning curve
Life's journey,
High speed, you skid and swerve
At times it will test your nerve
Then use your strength
You have saved in reserve
One day you'll be free
Released from this curse!

## Debris

These buildings are filled with
Dust and debris
Pigeons make any hole their resting place
Or their hiding place
Same for any child residing in this place
It isn't safe for a builder with a helmet
But we linger like a bad smell

The stench of some corners
Pierces our young senses
Ripped up porno mags
Blow in the wind
We never realised the danger
Syringes ready to sting like a nettle
We were falling like petals
Train depots were
Five star accommodation
Crazy kids running from the station

Security was tight
So many nights the bed bugs would bite
Old dusty drunks would give us a fright
With gangs we would fight

Derelict buildings
Once busy and vibrant
Now eerie and silent

I look around and see my friends
Making a bed like the pigeons
Hugging together for warmth
We call these all-nighters
Some call it home.

No breakfast in bed
No *Breakfast at Tiffany's*

You're kidding me
Never feeling the cold,
Was the kid in me
Just look what those days
Did to me

It's like they locked me in the boot
To get rid of me
Ridding me
Of my innocence
But harsh days make you strong
And tough
Tough like the security guards
Chasing us

But they can chase our dust
Bittersweet
But still good
Goodbye to my crazy childhood.

## Discover

There's a riot across the Big Smoke
And far beyond
Better hide in the town where you belong
Burning buildings
Thugs wielding bats and bricks
Makes you wish you were born rich
That you lived far out in the sticks
Hooded-up nutters
Don't let your curtain twitch
Because they will be certain to switch

Mindless scum
Brought up in a council house slum
It's all sticks and stones
But they don't break bones

Forget those name brand shoes
Or the big TV
Who cares about watching a film in 3D

The town ablaze
The odd shop stood tall
While the rest would fall
From this crooks' war

Do you know what never got it
Yeah the bookstore
The most important site on the high street
Those kids walked past
Like they were blinded
Read every book on that shelf
Become the brightest
They never gave a toss
In the slightest

The library too
Stood there
Like it was bullet proof

My little advice to you
Bury your head in those books
And discover the truth.

## One-Way Roads

Nine-to-five residents are oblivious
One of these kids
Will send them to oblivion
Hooded-up youths
Congregating at the pavilion
Middle-class thinking
These boys are silly kids
But they are like Billy the Kids
Pulling guns like John Wayne did

The thug life
The drug life
The mug life

Once you've made that decision
It's like pulling the plug on life
Getting sucked through a gaping hole
The devil raping your soul

Walking with your Walkman
Headphones blasting
These streets are whispering
These streets are talking
And taking
The youths
And making
And turning
Them into troops
Burning morals
To collect the loot
It's the truth, it's the truth

Walking with the street kid
Is like walking with the beast kid
You will end up deceased kid

Remember there's no glamour
Dying or residing in the slammer

No glamour
In champagne popping
Dom Perignon corks dropping
Cocaine snorting
Fast girls hawking

Tarted up five-feet-six-inch dolls
Come downs resemble six-foot holes
Like pirate flags
It's all skulls and bones
When you least expect it
You will face your foes
So please don't make this
A one way road ...

## Before It's Too Late

When I was eleven
I ran away from home
The streets I would roam
Lost in this big city
Alone

School went out the window
Along with honesty
Honestly I was a scallywag
Walking the rails with a paint bag
My feet I would drag

Fading smiles
Miles of walking and dodging the
Predators
Ready to snatch me

Had to be fast so they couldn't catch me
There was no relaxing
As the olders were taxing
Kidnapping and beating

Mistreated daily
It was enough to send me crazy
And to think I was just a baby
Those harsh times made me
A runaway, runaway

My friends ran away too
Derelict buildings
Shielding us from the cold
Lost souls
But we never asked for this path
And though sadness *was* rife
We still had laughs through the strife

Now where are you?

Stuck in the belly of the beast
Wondering why my friends are deceased
Was it 'cause of the London street blues?
Tell me why we self-abuse

You've got to love yourself
Don't mug yourself
You've got to reach higher
Throw water on Hell's fire

Are you and me different now?
Somehow you can't look in my eyes
What happened to you guys?

Is it too late to go back
And refuse to hate?
Are you destined for the prison gate?
You need to change your ways
Before it is too late!

## The Take Off

This goes out to the people born into poverty
Spending their last pound on the lottery
But giving out that negative energy
Is never going to see them paid properly

The government gangsters still taxing
While they sit back relaxing
Chopping benefits
Like a butcher
Forcing him to become a pusher
Her a hooker

I know life is what you make it
But most won't make it
So stop the lies
Stop the faking

This one goes out to the single mummy
Did you dream of this life
While your child was in your tummy
Just close your eyes
Pray better days are coming

To the elderly
Let me catch your attention
Does that petty pension
Make you feel like you are
Stuck in detention?
No heating
Lonely and freezing

To anyone else stuck in a struggle
Push your chest out
Show a little muscle
Grit your teeth through this hustle
And believe one day your dreams will
        Take off like a shuttle!

# JUDGE AND JURY

### Danger Dog

It's the rise of the danger dog
It's all scare tactics
Another child gets mauled
Situation getting drastic

Kids out of control
And so are the mutts they stroll with
Walking with sharp teeth
Is easier than a chiv
Or a big shank
Pit bull terrier as big as a tank

Cuddly puppies turn into killers
Get owned by scared kids
Drug-dealers
Bit like a lost child with no guidance
Turning to crime and violence

A man's best friend
Loyal until the end
It's all a fashion statement
The latest trend

Like a kid a puppy needs discipline
Keep aggression to the minimum
Watch the gangster-rap music spinning him
The Devil's winning him
Over
If you carry on it's over

Doggy's locked in a kennel
Awaiting its fate
Kid's locked in the penal
Waiting for his date

It's dog eat dog
It's war on the roads
So a child walking nervy and cold
Buys a dog
Big and bold
To protect his lost soul

But now they've both been captured
When robberies go wrong and the victims scattered
Someone's head gets fractured
Now the system's dealing with the matters
Before more blood gets splattered

It's the Dangerous Dogs Act and we bow to the Crown
Another kid in Feltham
Another Pit bull put down

Don't tell me I'm crazy
That I've not walked in these shoes
Scars across my head,
I've been a victim too
Dragged across the garden
My head used as a toy
I was nearly mauled to death as a boy

But I love dogs and I care for lost boys
You better care too before we're all destroyed!

## Falling Feathers

Times turned sour
The grey feathery mob
Got turfed from Trafalgar

They flew across London
And landed on tower after tower

I'm not just talking about the one controlled by the power
Yeah they got moved on like a Gipsy selling heather

Did you know tower blocks get watched
Through the eyes of a feather
Thunder above
Council housing tough like leather

Residents on the clock for CID
If someone knocks you ask to see ID
'Cos it's not the type of place you could call friendly

Residents being filmed by CCTV
The feather eyes up you're homely
Sees you in your security lonely

Many people wish they could vision
If only
Grey old crusty and dusty
Shedding feathers like drops of melting ice
Feathers drop from tower blocks and pry on your life
Watch your smiles, spot your strife
Feather floating so innocently
Some claiming it's spiritually

As the wind sways in gently what does it see?
Vietnamese planting cannabis trees

Falling gently
Past a kid's bedroom
Whilst high as the feather in the sky on Es
Experimenting with LSD

Two floors down shaven-headed men counting their proceeds
Dyed red cash from a robbery spree

Whilst these residents are living
In a grimy estate, crime ridden
An elderly man is forgiving

Preying through his stained glass
Looking as high up as Mars
He is blind to the kids patrolling in stolen cars
Give me a sign 'Oh Lord!'
Give me a sign
These kids are reaching the end of their tether
The elderly man reaches through his window
And catches a fallen feather

He cannot believe his eyes
How could he pray
And a sign fall from the skies

You see we see through different lenses
Some see lost kids
Some see the frenzied
Some see a feather
And never give a thought
Some commit crimes
And never get caught
Sometimes a falling feather
Spots many monsters
Sometimes a feather
Sees everything
'Cause a feather is your conscience.

### A Write Buzz

Some people jump from buildings
Like it's thrilling and fun
Some hunt elk with their rifle or gun
Graffiti was my kick
Spraying bricks with paint
Silver cans hitting panels of trains

Some do sport like running
Or racing
Some get thrills from paper-chasing
After Queen's faces
Until they're way out of breath
Chasing that money until their death

Some get excitement from going to the gym
Endorphins bringing good vibes
Some want to look good to hide what's inside

Some slag off others to make them feel nice
That's the same people suffering in life
We all love a thrill or a buzz from something
Whether it's watching banger cars bumping
Or a hurdler jumping
Or listening to house music thumping

I used to risk my life sky-diving
Would get a twisted buzz from nearly dying
But I've had enough from the buzz of fighting
Now I get my buzz from sitting here writing…

## Street Wise

Some boys played with toy cars
We played with metal bars
And set fires
On the way to becoming the lads
All the traits of a psychopath

They visited museums and studied from books
We bunked history and became hooked
Snotty-nosed kids slowly becoming crooks
They left school for work experience
We got involved in some serious shit

We were loving those times
Became popular and felt loved through our crimes
Standing on the roof screaming 'This town is mine!'

Unwise and troubled within
Life flashing past and fast through blinking
Dicing with death not thinking
Beers up the sleeve just drinking

Then the streets took him
Found not breathing
Yeah that's a family grieving
Trying to snatch you back while you were leaving

Learning harsh lessons
Crushing my young energy
Street life took a friend from me
Armed to fight the enemy

I closed down the town
When I took over the roof
Didn't give a shit if I fell
And that's the truth

Now I'm scarred-up
Tattooed, muscled with a gold tooth

No longer skinny
No longer featherweight
Like a heavyweight
That got knocked down
I jumped up to beat the count
To beat the clown
In front of me
Have the streets had enough of me
Or have I had enough of them
Enough of death and mayhem?

You see like a boat I was swaying
In rough seas
Hooded up in the alley
Yeah that was me
Now I'm at the Supreme Court
    with Ian Duncan Smith
Or on TV
Yeah live on ITV
Now I'm calm like the breeze
But look in my eyes
You'll always see the streets!

## Pointing Fingers

Is it a brave face
Living in this grave place
Is it voices stuck inside this mind
Was I born into a life of crime
A lovable rogue
Or a toe rag
The Asbo Kid, the scumbag?
A label, a statistic
Brain dead simplistic

Too much Xbox
Grand Theft Auto
Shooting at vexed cops
Wishing I could exit at the next stop

Kids weren't born bad
Weren't born mad
It's tears of joy for the baby boy at birth
Then innocence is stolen by this earth
Corrupted by the world's curse
And labels just makes a child worse

So next time you see a child spit
Swear or choke on a joint
Give it some thought
Before you stop and point.

## Hater

The heat rose up like a sauna
They visioned me as a goner

You see when most are down
They wanna pull on your legs

Sometimes you can only guess the stress
That manifests in their heads
But to hold onto jealous wishes
Has you playing with death's kisses

Stuck in your depression
The lesson is to never concentrate
On the badness
You will attract more sadness

But people are blind
You think you are alike
But they're different inside
I learnt these harsh lessons as a child

Come out of the darkness
Shine bright like torches
Run free like horses
But as I walk my roads
I walk cautious
Like a lady considering abortion

They say only the strongest survive
Some raise up their hands and see the light

You see hate consumed me
In this action packed movie

But I truly wasn't free
Until extinguishing demons from me

I understand that it's hard to show love
When you've been pushed and shoved

Beaten and broken
Has you lonely and hoping

Then hatred comes knocking
Has you cursing and mocking
Has you asking why your life seems so bleak
It's like you hide-and-seek
Turn the other cheek
Hating doesn't make you strong
It simply makes you weak

See I was you
And I am my life's creator
My life is now good
'Cause I'm no longer a hater.

## Many Hours to Think

To analyse
To travel back
Explore memories
Put the puzzle together

Some lie to themselves
How can you lie when trapped with your thoughts

Swearing you will change
Apologising to God

Asking for his help
With no shackles it's just excuses

Life is sprinting
No time to meditate

To just forget
When you are your greatest enemy

It's a daily battle
Reckless, writing regrets

Playing with emotions
Breaking hearts

A trail of destruction
Leaving your fingerprints on another soul

Self-destruction feels warm
Then it's gone

All gone
Face your demons

Outside you're tough but inside your screaming
Sometimes your strongest bond feels like the weakest link

Sometimes your greatest challenge is to rewind
Open up a can of dark energies

Your right hand reaching up to the sky
Is it God?

Is it blissful energies?
Are you leaving yourself open to attack?

Spin it three-sixty
Make it out of there in one piece

I'm watching you running
Stumbling

But you're gonna make it
Yes

You're gonna make it.

## Material Smiles

These material things really mean nothing
'Cause when you die you leave with nothing
Still I risk my freedom to possess sparkly things
Rolexes and diamond rings
Fresh trainers and designer jeans
Got to look fresh in front of my fellow beings
But that feeling ain't pure
Guess a part of me is just insecure

Corrupted by magazines, music vids and adverts
Gun to my head to release this hurt

But I just can't give in
'Cause beauty really starts from within
We're just a generation not thinking
Drug-taking, love-making and drinking

Destroying our souls, destroying our core
Forget Iraq, on my local streets there's a war

Colour-coded postcode battles
Rush hour squashed on the Tube like cattle
A heroin addict's body rattles

He used to be a father you know,
Wanted to watch his youngster grow

His missus was a hoe, drained him
    for every penny and pound
Till he broke down to the ground
Now he's lost and will never be found
But I walk past this punk and frown
Ain't got time for him
I'm shopping in this town

Bought some new Armani shades
Fresh t-shirt and shoes
I must admit I look better than you

I am me, I am you

I'm so many people
In this evil society where I exist
But when I'm alone
I'm lonely in anguish
Fuck this, material things don't mean shit
Just threw my clothes out the window
You can have them
Take back your magazines too
'Cause that ain't really me
But is it really you?

## Small Thing to a Giant

Was it fate that brought us close
Whilst you all gather may I raise a toast
To happiness and good health
Stability and wealth?

Can you understand the man within?
That's slightly damaged from past sins

Every day I am moving forward
I was so used to seeing hearses
And though I'm far from perfect
Through our off days
I still believe it's all worth it

Sometimes it's hard to take in
How I went from heart-breaking
To making a better path
I have to pinch myself and laugh

I have to look at my reflection
To see if it's still real
It all came in a flash
I splash cold water to wake up my eyes
I stare at myself and realise
I worked so hard for this
I work so hard to stay sane

But I've come too far to look back
Though negative thoughts try to knock
    me off track

I'm a father and a loving man
No longer a fighter with gloves on my
    hands
Sometimes I ask myself
'Was it all planned?'

This is not *Shawshank Redemption*
But it's that last word I mentioned

Some sort of spiritual awakening

That old being
They were breaking him
But then again
They were making him

You see you have to set your goals higher
Stay clear of the tyrants
And always remember
Pain is a small thing to a giant!

## Daddy Where Are You?

Daddy where are you?
I never knew you
I watched friends play football
With their dad

That was a feeling I never had
If daddy don't wanna know me
Then somehow I must be
Bad
That's why nobody trusts me

Daddy where are you?
When you know your father
Just dumped you
It made me angry,
I wanted to thump you
Basic reality is your decision
Made me hate myself
I found myself in prison

Daddy where are you?
I've learned many lessons in life
Let anger go, to free your strife
Forgiveness is the way to go
But how, when I know
Your other kids lived well
Having you around
While me and Jemma were in Hell
She went from bad man to bad man
I went from cell-to-cell

Daddy where are you?
Now as a man I have no-one to blame
But you should bow your head in shame
'Cause a little boy was innocent
But turned filthy
I had blood on my hands,
I was surely guilty

Daddy where are you?
Daddy where are you?

You see Dad that's my child calling
I'll never leave her
Catch her if she's falling
Last time you saw me I was crawling
As a man I find that appalling
But one thing I thank you for
You made me a fighter
A loving father who holds his daughter
    tighter

Daddy where are you?
Baby girl I'm right here
I'll wipe your tears
Yeah we'll laugh till we cry
Like that time we tried to fly
That cheap kite
You see baby, you have been my future
Remember
I'm a natural father
Because I never had a tutor!

**Actors**

Crime actors
Start believing they're gangsters
Puffing out chests
Parading their feathers
Alter egos
Living a life of make believe
But they're far from
Old Bailey bandits
More like misfits
Never on the level of Al Pacino
Or De Niro
False celebrity illusions
Cocaine burning nostrils
Low budget British crime thrillers
Have many actors believing they're killers
Fame does funny things
Tests personalities
Turns people ugly
Were they not beautiful before?
Actors
Actors
Dramatic energies
See dramas played out
See actors lose their once ordinary character
Don't recognise the road they grew on
You are inside the television
You're gone
You're gone.

# INDEX OF FIRST LINES

## Index of First Lines

'This is simply 100% raw talent being unleashed right from the start... This book is a must-read for the prison population, academics and politicians': *Inside Time*

Discover many hidden clues to *Street Crhymes* in Justin Rollins' acclaimed true story of growing up (and out of crime) in south-London.

## The Lost Boyz: A Dark Side of Graffiti
## by Justin Rollins

With a Foreword by Noel 'Razor' Smith

A rare first-hand account of disaffected youth. Contains countless lessons for young people who might be attracted to crime (and anyone involved with them socially or professionally). Aged just fourteen, the author went from being a bullied child to leader of a group of London street kids involved in graffiti-tagging and other crimes. Eventually given a custodial sentence for an attack on the London Underground, Justin Rollins became determined to steer other young people away from such a life.

'An unforgettable story of a violent and disturbed young man, who, despite spiralling out of control, is anchored by his friendships and the power of his gang community': *Social Work With Groups*

Paperback | ISBN 978-1-904380-67-2 | 2011 | 176 pages

**www.WatersidePress.co.uk**